3 <u>00</u>

D1450944

An Academy Called
PAIN

An Academy Called
PAIN

Paige Cothren

The
Remarkable ability
of Head Coach John Vaught,

Enabled by committed
    assistants - - -
Tempered by the
    times - - -

Fanned the smoldering
    coals of our
    adolescent immaturity

Into the burning flames
of athletic manhood

~ Paige Cothren

CONTENTS

PREFACE

After *Walk Carefully Around the Dead* was published in October 1998, many former Ole Miss football players contacted me with comments. Gratefully, the unanimous consensus of opinion was positive. Judged in the affirmative by those who "know" means a great deal to me.

With one voice, however, they proclaimed words similar to these, "How I wish you could have written about the time ... etc., etc.," and then they would tell me the story.

I agreed with every one of them.

For example, while I was signing books at Lemuria Book Store in Jackson, an old teammate, Don Barkley, sat down next to me at the table and related the story entitled, "What do you THINK I'm Running Here?" Everyone standing in line listened to the tale, as I, apologetically, stopped the signing. After Don finished and the laughter subsided, at least ten of us agreed it should be recorded.

Well, now it is – and many, many others like it.

Numerous gracious and appreciative people have asked if I planned to write a sequel to *Walk Carefully Around the Dead*. The format of *Walk Carefully*, I think prohibits a sequel, in that a sequel further develops and clarifies a story. *Walk Carefully*, on the other hand, is a collection of stories, so although technically a sequel may be impossible to produce, a continuation of funny stories certainly isn't.

An Academy Called Pain, I hope, will be as funny and meaningful to you as dozens of you have asserted to me that *Walk Carefully* was!

INTRODUCTION

AGAIN – A WARNING

Please be informed again, as you were in *Walk Carefully Around the Dead*, that many of the yarns contain indelicate language at the best and lascivious wording at the worst. The less indecent words, like damn and hell will, unlike in *Walk Carefully Around the Dead*, be spelled out for easier reading; the more extreme words will be identified by the first letter and the last letter with dots in between. I hope the full words aren't offensive nor the narrative thereby rendered boring.

One might properly ask, "Paige, why include indecorous words in the book at all – why not just replace them with synonyms?" Good questions! Simple answer!

Truth and promise!!

I want to preserve the truth, and I promised those who related the stories to me that I would carefully attempt to record them as told.

In the late forties, in the fifties, and the early sixties, profanity on college gridirons was not considered to be profane!

I don't know why!! Coaches just "cussed." Moms and Dads knew it; school administrators knew it; fans knew it; preachers knew it; and the players knew it, expected it, received it, and laughed about it. Our overwhelming joy in being at Ole Miss and our "innocent naivety" (redundancy yielding to emphasis) accepted it without resentment. In some cases it might even have been welcomed. Attention of any kind from a coach on a field of unlimited scholarships might be greeted with appreciation from an aspiring athlete who secretly wondered if a mentor even knew his name.

One of my teammates recently exclaimed, "I was a

senior at Ole Miss before I found out my name wasn't "damn you!" I'M ALMOST CERTAIN HE WAS JOKING!

* * * * *

In Nineteen Forty-five, the Second World War ended and a nation which had been completely preoccupied with fear and concern suddenly burst out of that encompassing darkness into the enveloping light of freedom and joy! At the news of Japan's surrender, thousands of American church bells rang and victory parades suddenly exploded upon the streets of every town with people pouring out of businesses, homes and schools. This nation's industrial might which had swamped the enemy with unlimited hardware and weaponry, began the process of beating the swords of the Second World War into plowshares.

And our boys came home!

Would you permit me to quote from my introduction in *Walk Carefully Around the Dead?*

"World War II ended in Nineteen Forty-Five and this nation mutated into a NEOS COSMOS, a New World, of celebration and ecstacy. Fear acquiesced to joy, and love of life, which many doubted they would ever experience again, suddenly erupted. The negativism produced by more than four years of war yielded to positivism, a belief that life would get better. With the G.I. Bill and other Federal aid programs, higher education became a possibility for many young Americans and college became a center for the positivism. "Bring on the good times," we expected. "I'm a lover not a fighter," became as much a by-word in peace as "Kilroy was here" had been in war ...."

And our boys came home!

For Ole Miss, eight of these "boys" were Coaches John Vaught, Buster Poole, Bruiser Kinard, Junie Hovious, John Cain, Wobble Davidson, head scout Tom Swayze, trainer Doc Knight, and a dressing room full of players led by All-

Americans Charlie Conerly and Barney Poole. The Coaches brought back authority and structure, and the players learned an attitude of discipline, submission to authority and endurance of pain. Together, they launched the football program at Ole Miss like an illumination projectile propelled from a 155 mm howitzer exploding above a Pacific beach, and the light reflecting from their successes radiated from every sports page in America. A football program which had lounged, for the most part, in mediocrity before the war now stood poised like a Roman Centurion, sword in hand, ready to carve up all who challenged.

The militaristic coaches assumed control of the Rebel football program in Nineteen Forty-Seven and with Conerly passing, Poole receiving, they promptly won the SEC Championship. As a result of Coach Vaught's pre-season agreement, their enfeebled reward consisted of playing TCU in the first and only Delta Bowl in Memphis. Ole Miss' victory did little to assuage their disappointment at being kept out of the Sugar Bowl. Coach Vaught later asserted, "I made a mistake by agreeing to play in a bowl before the season started. I'll never do that again!" — and he never did.

SUBMISSION TO AUTHORITY

The Nineteen Forties, Nineteen Fifties, and early Nineteen Sixties were years marked by submission to authority without consideration. By that I mean submission was a lifestyle, inherited from the preceding generation, without question. It was not an individual choice, not before the Mid-Sixties. The thought that our coaches possessed less than rights of life and death over us never trespassed our minds. We subjectively believed that they owned the right to work us as hard as they wanted, without restraint even to and beyond the point of death. We hoped they wouldn't, but more than once believed they had! The practices were conducted as often, as long, and as hard as the coaches desired, and each day, when the workouts finally ended, usually well after dark, many of us lay on the field for lengthy periods of time deciding whether to try to make it to the dressing room or remain there and die. Some days, the choice wasn't all that easy.

Submission to the authority of the Coaches, for us, wasn't an option. If we wanted to play football at Ole Miss, we submitted; if we weren't willing to submit, we experienced very short football careers in Oxford.

Enduring pain wasn't an option either. Due to limited substitution, discussed fully in *Walk Carefully Around the Dead*, players were forced to play when hurt. To come out of the game meant you could not re-enter it until the next quarter.

Besides, we didn't want to let the opposition know that they had made us suffer!

CHAPTER I

MAKE IT HURT!

I've been this way all my life – I dislike doubting the acumen of my superiors – or the wisdom of the culture into which I'm born. I don't really know why. I suppose the Nineteen-Forties culture taught me to submit – therefore, out of respect for it, I do.

For the most part, culture provides mankind with a wonderful agency! Many profitable qualities may be imparted to us through it – emotional and physical security, self-worth, a sense of belonging. Subconsciously, I think, human nature craves clearly identifiable areas of acceptable behavior, which may only be established by the installation of limits to that conduct. Culture provides those arenas. Men and women born into a certain society, who grow up in it, and reside in it, tend to live within its limits. The law of the land, commingling with an historical, moral principle, like the Judeo/Christian ethic upon which America constructed its jurisprudence, establishes the boundaries, dividing lines between acceptable and unacceptable behavior.

Cultures, however, often find themselves subject to alterations, changes engendered by certain stimuli – selfishness, pleasure, desires, social and racial readjustments, the entertainment industry, the media – to mention a few. As behavioral limits expand outward, which they almost always do in order to reject no one, deportment once disallowed by society becomes acceptable.

Today, trench coats, swastikas, and X's, broadcasting death to people of other races, religions, or cultures, may be worn, without recourse, into the classrooms of public schools, all in the name of "personal freedom," a "freedom" which in the final analysis, tends to enslave, at the very least, the emotions. Emotions then control behavior.

A different culture, in an earlier time, taught a contrasting standard. I know – I was there.

It was the last day of school, 1952, my junior year at old Crosby High. I was class president.

Assembling the entire class immediately outside the front door of the high school building fifteen minutes before the first bell, I announced to the troops my strategy for the last day of school.

"TROOPS – ATTENSHUT! AT EASE!"

"Shoes and socks – TAKE OFF!", I commanded in a military voice patterned as closely as I could to that of a Second World War drill sargeant.

"MEN – ROLL UP PANTS LEGS!"

"Form a single line facing me – HERE!"

"ATTENSHUT!"

"RIGHT FACE! FORWARD, MARCH!"

I marched my company into English Class, taught by disciplinarian, Mr. James Thompson, the man who made me learn how to diagram sentences, the principal of the school.

"Hut – two – three – four – HUT – TWO – three – four!"

"Company – HALT."

"Company — be SEATED!"

"Sir," I reported to Captain Thompson, "Your troops are barefoot, seated, and eager to learn!"

Captain Thompson wasn't smiling.

"That's fine, Sargeant Cothren," responded the teacher, "now call your troops to attention – march them back outside – have the boys roll down their pants legs to the appropriate height – have everyone re-dress – and march them back to the door of this classroom. Stop them there and I'll take over."

16

"YES, SIR!"

I obeyed my officer's commands.

"The troops are lined up in the hall, SIR," I reported a few minutes later.

"That's good, Sargeant. Now beginning with you, one by one, march them to my desk, and command them to bend over. Each will be awarded a combat medal, one lick to the posterior as hard as I can swing the paddle."

So – I took my lick and one by one, I filed my incensed soldiers, girls and all, to the awards platform – where each of them court marshaled and executed me with slanted eyes. When the troops had received their medals, we pledged allegiance to the flag, rubbed our rear ends, and took our seats. By the decree of the culture, the captain, toward whom no ire extended, was clearly in control.

That summer, I, toward whom lots of ire extended, transferred to Natchez High School in Natchez.

* * * * *

Just as submission wasn't, pain wasn't an option upon the Ole Miss football field, or in the dorm, or at "Freshman meetings."

Seems like I've been hurting all my life! It started with growing up in the Poole family, around uncles Ray and Buster and cousins Phillip and Jackie. Uncle Barney and cousins Oliver, Flemming and Leslie exercised mercy, probably balancing the others' maltreatment of me.

Ray, whom the relatives then called "Bady," for the reason discussed in *Walk Carefully Around the Dead*, page 202, became my major antagonist. His ability to irritate nieces and nephews knew no boundaries, and few minutes existed when his devious mind failed to conceive and execute some annoyance. Because I grew up in the same house with him, the only nephew to do so, his access to me was constant and so were his provocations. To make matters worse, he viewed me more as a younger brother than a nephew, though in truth, it probably wouldn't have mattered. When, therefore, I struck back, as I often did, it usually resulted in major recompense.

In the Fall of 1949, Crosby High School won the State Class B football championship with a 12 won, 0 loss record. The less-than-wealthy school awarded the lettermen with very nice felt and leather football jackets, one of the few times it was ever able to do so. At age 14, I was the starting right guard.

That same fall toward the end of his third season with the New York Giants, Ray suffered a broken leg. With a cast on it, he and his new wife, Wanda, came home before the NFL season ended. It was the middle of December.

I can't remember how a 14-year old boy who lived in the middle of the Homochitto National Forest ever saw a miniature golf course, but somewhere, somehow I did. So in the summer of 1949 I decided to build one on a grassy area just outside Mama Poole's front yard fence. I scraped the grass off the fairways with a hoe, delicately manicuring every bump until each was perfectly smooth. I used bricks and dirt berms to offer obstacles along with bowls filled with water. I designed dog-legs to the left and right; I elevated a few greens and several tees, and I played on my 18-hole masterpiece every waking minute. I didn't want to hoe the garden or cut bean sticks or slop the hogs or feed the chickens. I wanted only to play golf on my miniature golf course, and I became very proficient at it, the Homochitto Champion, the master of my imaginative creation, where late afternoons, Saturdays and Sunday afternoons often found numerous relatives engaged in vicious elimination tournaments with both younger and older cousins, adults and neighbors. No one could beat me. I buried small rocks picked from the gravel road in every fairway, leaving only an invisible part protruding above ground, just enough impediment to turn an unsuspecting golf ball, and I remembered where I cached every one of them. I was invincible, untouchable – until my par-golfing Uncle Ray, cast and all, came home.

It was a Sunday afternoon. Twenty-five or so relatives were gathered on my diminutive design. Everyone had been eliminated but Ray and me. We were to play 18 more holes, a play-off, to determine the reigning conqueror.

I knew it wouldn't be easy. My convalescent competitor had discovered my secret, submerged advantages. Besides, he was an excellent putter (and still is). I had my hands full – but the Poole money lay on me.

The game was close, vacillating back and forth, as I gained a stroke and then lost it. After 17 holes we were tied. On the final hole I putted first.

Number 18 was a long par 2. I had half-buried two bricks about two feet in front of the hole leaving a six-inch opening between them. To par the hole the ball needed to roll through the opening. Mine did, and I tapped my second putt in for a par.

My unruffled relative wasn't quite as fortunate. His first putt hit one of the bricks and bounced back about 12 inches. Still he had a shot, his ball having stopped directly in line with the inside of one of the bricks. The angle was difficult, and he would have to be careful not to hit the brick again.

I decided as additional security, to place a hex on my rival. The most powerful curse in the 1940's culture of South Mississippi was the "Yankees on you" one, so I stood just beyond the hole, leaned over so my head was directly above it, opened my right hand with the palm down, making circular motions and whispering, "Yankees on you – Yankees on you."

It worked!

He missed!

I won! — the golf match – not the fight.

When Ray missed and I laughed, he slammed his putter into my immaculate fairway and drove about six inches of it up into my smirking face.

I attacked, more for destroying fairway 18 than for dirt in my face. I head-butted him, as hard as a 175 pound starting right guard for a State Champion Class B football team could. My friend the cast, and I put him on the ground, mostly the cast.

The fight had just begun.

As my stunned uncle fell, handicapped by his encased leg, he grabbed for me, gathering a handful of leather, and he separated my left green leather sleeve from the grey felt as I fell on top of him. I had been emboldened by the fact that I could out-run him, but now the contest shifted in his favor as both of us sprawled on the ground. Quickly he rolled on top of me, turned me face down to the ground, placed his two knees on my grappling arms and facing my feet with his body resting upon my neck, he proceeded to test the metal of his putter against my exposed rear end.

My frantic screams attracted no interest from my kinfolk competitors, some of whom had started a new game on hole number one, and some of whom were nonchalantly walking toward the house. Neither did they extract concern from the numerous relatives who were in the house. But they did lure the solicitude of Ray's bride, Wanda, who sprinted out of the house censuring my flagellating restrainer. A few seconds later the putter was in my new aunt's hand, Ray was climbing off me, and Wanda had made a friend forever.

Glancing over his shoulder as he walked toward the

house, a cousin voiced the thoughts of all of them. "First time I ever saw ANYONE make Bady do ANYTHING!"

"Yep," another relative speculated, "she may be fixin' to TAME him!"

A few minutes later Ray's mother, my grandmother Mama Poole, casually summarized the ignoble event. "Now Bady, you ought'n to have torn his coat."

No one remembered my posterior – it was expendable!

PAIN – A FRIEND?!?

I grew up getting my rear-end attacked every time I misbehaved and then again on my birthdays. When I was 12, a kicked football slammed into my left eye from five yards away and for two weeks, the doctor thought I might lose it. The pain was awesome. When I was 13, I had my right forefinger folded back onto my wrist, and the knuckle shattered and scattered around third base. The doctors thought I might lose the finger, but three operations and a steel pin later, it was saved. The pain was searing.

I played high school football in a leather helmet and paper thin pads. Every contact sent shock waves through my entire body like ripples from a rock thrown into a placid pond. Once when I was 14, I made the tackle on the opening kickoff and played an entire football game "out" on my feet. When the game ended, I was left standing in the middle of the field, crying because I didn't know where I was. My Dad led me off the field, and my head hurt for a week. I probably had a concussion, but folks knew little about those back then, so I practiced every day the following week and played the next Friday night. The knot behind my left ear still swells and hurts, and when I suffer occasional bouts of vertigo it seems to emanate from that spot.

When I was 14 and playing adult summer baseball with the "Pooles of Pooletown," a 25-year old opposing pitcher stuck a fastball into my left eye, because I kept waiting for the pitch to curve. My head hit the ground a full two seconds before the ball came down, almost to third base. When I woke up at the clinic, Mother told me I said it "smarted some." I don't remember.

Then in 1953 I went to Ole Miss to play football. The helmets were hard, but the pads were still thin and made out of a material which conducted shockwaves from the point of impact straight through the flesh into the bones, causing the birth of a by-word: "I never took a lick that didn't hurt."

At Ole Miss I suffered freshmen meetings, which I will discuss later; the M-Club initiation; broken bones; displaced fingers; broken teeth; knee operations; and playing LSU, which offered its own brand of torture.

For four years, pain was a daily companion.

Pro-football in the fifties and sixties offered more of the same.

I still experience residual pain daily as do many of you, I suspect. Let's see, my left knee stays swollen and throbs incessantly; my right heel pulsates with the pain of Achilles tendons ripped in football practice; and my left shoulder offers to the throbbing confusion a torn rotator cup, which at some point should undergo surgery. Add to all of that, ten root canals, hernia surgery and prostate cancer, among various other maladies.

My cup of discomfort overflows with the wine of torment. Thank goodness for the 1950's teaching that, "Aw, Paige, a little pain is good for you." Otherwise I might think physical affliction could disadvantage me some way.

Anyway, such was the mentality of athletic life at Ole

Miss when I arrived. Pain would separate the men from the boys. Ignoring it and pressing on would lift one's self from the degradation of commonality into the glory of selective excellence!! It would prove the power of mind over matter and elevate the levels of desire and determination!! It would mandate manhood and consummate courage!!

And it would win football games! In limited substitution, the team which could "play through pain" added points to the scoreboard.

Our coaches, Head Coach John Vaught; Offensive Line Coach Bruiser Kinard; Defensive Line Coach Buster Poole; Offensive Back Coach John Cain; Defensive Back Coach Junie Hovious; Freshman Coach Wobble Davidson; Red-shirt Coach Ray Poole; Trainer Doc Knight; Head Scout Tom Swayze; Athletic Director Tad Smith; and Country Graham, Assistant coach; had played with that mentality, served in the armed forces during the Second World War with that perception, and came to coach at Ole Miss with that belief. All of us who played under Vaught and his staff became recipients of their views.

Total, unquestioned submission to authority and the "friendship" of pain formed a stage upon which many extremely funny episodes occurred. *An Academy Called Pain* continues the remembrance of them from *Walk Carefully Around the Dead.*

I hope you enjoy — !

By the way, I've been asked many times if I would "do it again – suffer all that pain in order to play football."

Certainly! I know of no source of intellectual wisdom which teaches that an idiot ceases to be an idiot just because of a little physical pain!

CHAPTER II

THE LOWLY FRESHMAN

INTRODUCTION

I knew a lot about Ole Miss before I actually enrolled as a student in its hallowed halls. I had studied with great interest its history; I was as familiar with its athletic program as a 17-year old boy could be, eight of my close relatives having preceded me to Hemingway Stadium; and I knew every member of its coaching staff personally.

I also understood a limited amount about being a freshman, about upper-classmen's "hazing." I knew about it intellectually, but of course, before I arrived on campus as a real live freshman, I could not have known it experientially. Nowhere else did intellectual knowledge and experiential knowledge stand farther apart than in me the day before I became a freshman at Ole Miss.

One of my first lessons upon dismounting from my steed of experiential ignorance was learning that the word "haze" inadequately described the activity, at least in the Forties and Fifties. For one thing it failed to delineate whether the enterprise assessed a physical or an emotional disposition, or both. Before the unnerving sound of the first wide paddle swung by a muscled upper-classman against my quaking rear-end had cleared the air, I fully understood the issue, experientially. It was both, and then some! Obviously, while I was being flagellated, the physical pain preempted everything else. All other times found me agonizing over the next scourging, certain to occur some time the following day. And those informal individualistic whippings didn't even include the "organized" freshman meetings.

FRESHMAN MEETINGS

At least twice a week football upper-classmen announced freshman meetings — little fun-filled, social gatherings whereby high school heroes were suddenly slammed back to humility and veteran athletes could exercise their indignation toward those who had come to replace them. After the first assembly, all freshmen on scholarship hated the words, usually bellowed out by a varsity football player during supper in the athletic cafeteria.

"FRESHMAN MEETING – TONIGHT," spoiled the taste of the most succulent, inch-thick, choice t-bone steak cooked to perfection and staled the softest most butter-saturated French bread. The dreaded words spread pepper upon the pecan pie and salted the vanilla ice cream. Any joy and happiness which might have formed in a freshman's heart through the day was extricated and destroyed under the affirmation. The toughest, most courageous linemen wanted to break and run, which some did.

The gatherings served a purpose we were told. I'm still not sure, other than perhaps replacing a little arrogance with a touch of humility. I suppose they made us tougher. They certainly established a clear chain of command and the meetings most assuredly prompted ordinary students to respect athletes as they drove and walked by in silent, reverential awe, momentarily delighted for having been spared athletic ability.

A street, a grassy incline, and a parking lot lay, in that order, between the athletic cafeteria and Garland Hall where upper-classmen and a few select freshmen lived. After supper the vigorous veterans would command the fearful and trembling freshmen of all sports to sit on the grassy bank. Then one by one our names were called, and we were brought down to the street, where we stood at attention facing the others. Our high school exploits and honors would then be remembered; our arrogance would be observed; and our attitudes examined; whereupon we were told to grab our ankles. Depending upon the accumulative perception of the unimpressed upper classmen, we inherited from one to ten licks with a paddle as hard as the wielder could swing it.

Amazingly, my Uncle Buster accounted for many of my licks. Almost every time he reproved a varsity player, which was often, the censured one paddled me. "Well, who do we have here? I do believe it's our high school hero and All-American, Unca' Bus. Unca' Bus, this will teach you to stay off my ass!"

SLAVES

For there to be a slave-master, there must be a slave. Each freshman athlete served a master, or two. That meant the first-year man was compelled to perform any task his master or masters desired, whenever he or they desired it.

For one lagging year, reticent freshmen developed abilities we never dreamed we would be forced to generate. We discussed ways to harden the skin and flesh of our tails. Would rubbing salt into the area every day eventually do it? Maybe tuf-skin, that sticky, smelly ointment from Doc Knight's training room would help!

Evading upper-classmen became a skill which some freshmen seemed to master and some didn't. We learned to laugh softly, talk quietly, and spend a lot of time away from the dorm.

One of the most heavily-recruited high school football players ever to enroll at Ole Miss was Bobby (Slick) McCool, a big fast fullback from Cleveland, Mississippi, to be featured in another chapter of this book – To Be Initiated. Slick, an All-State, All-South, and high school All-American, earned the outstanding player award in the 1952 High School All-American game held at that time in Memphis.

The powerful running back appeared as a freshman at Ole Miss that fall wearing blue jeans, his High School All-American t-shirt, a wide leather belt with "BIG SLICK" emblazoned across the back, a big confident grin, a "cocky" attitude, and a loud voice. By October of his freshman year, the t-shirt, the arrogance and the booming voice were gone. The upperclassmen wore the wide leather belt out on his posterior.

In losing all that, Slick learned how to be an upperclassman. In the fall of '53, he ordained me his slave, an appointment made more harrowing for me because we played the same position. A day or two later sophomore Billy Kinard joined him affording me two malevolent masters, both of whom possessed strong right arms and disconcerting attitudes toward me.

In September, I faced a hellish year, but without the sense to know it. I never became proficient at evasion, even though I learned how to press my back against the wall and slide tip-toeing up or down the dormitory stairs. By the end of the year, I had, however, progressed some in the art of keeping my mouth shut, and exhibiting humility, however contrived it might have been.

MY TWO AUNTS

I was, at the same time, one of the most unfortunate and fortunate fellows ever to play football for the Ole Miss Rebels; the former because I labored under two extremely attentive uncles who coached me, Buster and Ray Poole; the latter because both were married to compassionate women, Anna and Wanda, who looked after my welfare.

Beginning my freshman year, Buster, influenced by

Anna, offered me a proposition which I could not refuse. I would baby-sit their young children, Jimbo and Joanna one night, and receive the use of Buster's small yellow Chevrolet one night – one for one. Of course, my uncle kept the car from me during football season, but he allowed my salary to accrue. By January 2, I had accumulated ten or twelve usages. Buster meticulously recorded the transactions in a small note-book.

I received no freebies – but I did get food. Anna always left cake or pie and reminded me that milk was in the refrigerator. I found the beer on my own, drinking no more than one can. I figured Buster would notice.

Anna and later Wanda, when Ray came onto the staff my junior year, also attended to my social life, a positive endeavor from my vantage point. They seemed to know all the girls on campus and offered welcome advice regarding whom I should date.

"Paige, I have a name for you."

"What do you mean, Aunt Anna?"

"Don't call me aunt! You're a college student now, and I won't have a college student calling me aunt!"

"Ok, aunt – ah – Anna, what do you mean?"

"I know a girl you ought to date."

It was the middle of September 1953. I was a fresh-man, and the other students had just arrived on campus. Football players had been there for almost three weeks, and we were ready to look at something other than hairy, male tor-sos, so I ingested Anna's suggestion quickly and enthusiasti-cally. It was her first one to me.

"Her name is Shirley Wagner."

"How do you know her?" I quizzed.

"We're both from Grenada. I've known her all her life."

"Is she good-lookin'?"

"Why is THAT the first thing boys ask about girls?" demanded Anna. "Doesn't anything else matter to you?"

"Yeah, are they rich?"

I wanted to suggest one other inclination, but I didn't have the guts. If Anna hadn't killed me, Buster would have–!"

"Good looking and rich, huh? What about personality? Isn't that important to you?"

"Yes'm, I guess so."

"To answer your question, Shirley is beautiful, very nice, and she has a great personality. You won't be sorry you called her."

I called her – a week later. I waited too long.

I asked Shirley for a date after Saturday's game. She already had one. Friday night before the game? She had one. Next Saturday night? She had one. What about that Friday night? She had one already.

"When is the first Friday or Saturday night you don't have a date, Shirley?"

"About the first of November."

"Dang," I exclaimed. "Do you date during the week?"

"Yes, but freshman girls have to be in by 8:30, you know!"

"8:30? Why?"

"I don't know," she confessed, "it's just the rules."

"When is your first week-night opening?"

Shirley hesitated before answering. I hoped she was looking at her calendar.

"Two weeks from tomorrow night."

"That's 15 days!"

"I know," she responded, "but I would love to go out with you then, Paige, if you like–!"

"I like, I like! See you at 7:00? We won't have time to do anything but walk to the grill!"

"See you then, Paige."

The Date – Almost!

"Damn, I hope we don't have a freshman meeting tonight," I whispered to my roommate, Jerry McKaskel, who, like me, was from Natchez. I whispered so no upper-class-man could hear me.

"I hope we don't have one ANY night. Why just tonight?" Jerry quietly asked.

"I have a date with Shirley Wagner."

"Finally got here, huh?"

"Finally got here!"

Reflecting back, it was hilarious watching freshman football players try to slip unnoticed out of the athletic cafeteria. If no freshman meeting had been called, masters usually ambushed the slaves for some task, cleaning up the room, washing socks and underwear, running errands. I waited until Slick and Billy had left the cafeteria.

"Let's go," I murmured to McKaskel.

We entered Garland Hall on the opposite end from my two masters' rooms. We had almost gotten to our room on the third floor when I heard McCool's loud sophomoric voice.

"Cothren, get your freshman ass down here."

"Aw man, I can't believe this," I groaned, as Jerry quickly darted into the room, deposited his books and sprinted down the stairs to freedom, which waited outside.

I trudged toward Slick's room.

"What do you want?" I asked. Billy was sitting in a chair, Slick looking in his closet.

"Freshman, you want your butt whipped right now?" It's not 'what do you want?', but 'WHAT CAN I DO FOR YOU, SIR!' Understand?"

"Yes, sir."

"Then say it right."

"What can I do for you, sir?"

"That's better! You can wash our socks and underwear."

"Right now?"

"Hell yes, right now – when do you think?"

"Maybe after 8:30?" I pleaded.

"Why 8:30, freshman?"

"I have a date!

"You have a date? Did you hear that Billy? Cothren has a date!"

I looked at Billy. He was snarling.

"Who in hell would date you?" he asked.

"Shirley Wagner."

"Shirley Wagner!?! Shirley Wagner wouldn't give you the time of day."

"She gave me a date tonight!"

"Freshman, when I say she won't date you, she won't

date you. You're gettin' smart! Grab your ankles."

I grabbed my ankles. Three loud "pops" and a ton of discomfort later I raised back up rubbing my rear end, trying to extinguish the pain.

"You can't go," Slick declared. "You gotta' wash our socks and underwear."

"Ya'll, please! I'll wash 'em after 8:30."

"You'll wash 'em when we tell you to wash 'em, Freshman. Get with it."

"I need to call Shirley and tell her I can't come."

"I'll call her for you," Billy offered.

"Please let me call her," I begged.

"Freshman, every time you open your smart mouth, you'll get one more lick after you get through washin'!"

Billy left the room to call Shirley on the pay phone down the hall. As I scrubbed the socks and underwear in the lavatory, I could hear him talking.

"Shirley, Paige asked me to call you and tell you he's been thinking it over and he's decided he doesn't want to date you after all. He doesn't think you are either nice or pretty, so he asked me to call and tell you he isn't coming tonight or any night."

I heard him hang up the phone. I could have killed them both, but I restrained that pleasant thought from surfacing onto my distraught face.

I finished my washing about 8:00; took my ten licks with the paddle; hustled back up to my room where I pulled my bloody underwear off; doctored my wounds; and called Shirley.

She understood!

I finally got my date with Shirley, however, much later, and we became good friends. Shirley Wagner Crawford, wife of my teammate Eddie Crawford, present Assistant Athletic Director at Ole Miss. We remain good friends until this day.

Funny thing about friendships created in college. They seem to remain a lifetime. Billy Kinard and Slick McCool are still my friends, although I don't get to see them often. So it is with one of our other teammates, Gene Dubuisson.

TELL ME IT ISN'T SO!!

On Saturday afternoon, December 19, 1998, I was autographing *Walk Carefully Around the Dead*, at Favorites Book Store in Ocean Springs. I had been signing for about an hour when I looked up into the face of a tall, powerfully built man. He sported a crew-cut and a carefully manicured beard, both turned grey apparently by the passage of time. The twinkle in his eyes unmasked the sternness of his face, and they seemed to deepen as he gazed down at me. A little uncomfortably I blurted out, "How do you do, sir?"

"You don't even know me, do you?"

"Boy," I replied, trying to conceal embarrassment, "you really look familiar."

"I'm Gene Dubuisson."

"Duby!" The word exploded from my mouth, at the same time my coiled legs propelled me from my chair and around the table, almost turning it over. I bear-hugged him at the same moment he bear-hugged me. Tears, which I quickly wiped away in hopes no one had seen them, welled up in my eyes.

"It's been 42 years," he declared. "We haven't seen each other in 42 years."

"I know! We've all missed seeing you."

Someone called the local paper and in a few minutes a photographer, sports writer was snapping a picture and writing the story. A little later with a degree of discomfort, I signed his book.

"To Gene – Ole Miss' greatest center on Ole Miss' greatest team." I played with him on the 1955 SEC Championship team which won the Cotton Bowl following that season.

As Duby prepared to leave, I announced to everyone standing around, "Look, the reason I didn't recognize him is because he played center and I played fullback. If he had turned around and bent over I think I would have known him."

"I'd better go," Duby laughed, "my wife's waiting for me in the car."

"Can I meet her?"

"Certainly."

As we walked out of Favorites and neared the car, her head turned toward us, and a giant smile spread across her lovely face. Gene introduced us, and Sissy extended her right hand through the open window. Grasping mine, she looked through her smile pleadingly into my eyes.

"Tell me it isn't so!"

"What?"

"Tell me it isn't so!" she repeated.

I looked at Gene.

"Remember my senior year at Ole Miss, Paige, when I was circumcised?"

"Yes, yes! I had forgotten about that!"

"And do you remember what I made Tar Baby do?"

For the first time in 42 years I remembered what Duby made Tar Baby do for him after his surgery. In the middle of the Ocean Springs street, I doubled over with uncontrolled laughter.

"Tell me it isn't so!"

"Sorry, Sissy, it is SO!!"

Tar Baby was Gayle Bowman's nickname. He was a small halfback from Gene's home town, Pascagoula, and he was a freshman when Duby was a senior. The two had known each other all their lives. Tar Baby belonged to Gene and also to Earl Blair, like Gayle, a half-back from Pascagoula. Freshmen football players were slaves in the 50's and both the upper-classmen were unmerciful to Tar Baby, even for that day and time.

When Gene arrived back at Garland following surgery, he called Tar Baby into his room.

"Freshman, I've got to take a shower. Pull your clothes off, pick up that drinkin' glass and follow me." Gene then slowly and meticulously arose from his bed and undressed. With great care he moved ever so slowly down the hall toward the shower. A nude 160 pound halfback followed – with a glass in his hand.

A few minutes later someone yelled from the shower room. "Ya'll come see this – you won't believe it – Hurry!"

Football players headed out of their rooms, down the hall and to the shower. I'm surprised, even with time, that I had forgotten the scene!

Standing in the shower was Duby and bending over facing him was Tar Baby, the glass in his hand firmly encompassing Duby's penis. As Duby rotated under the water, Tar Baby in chorus, frantically turned with him.

"Freshman," the upper-classmen threatened, "You let

one drop of water hit my ----, and I'm gonna destroy your scrawny little ass."

A very serious Tar Baby made certain that no water found the target. The collective mirth at the shower door diminished none of Tar Baby's determination.

"Tell me it isn't so!"

If any college friendship ever failed, Duby's and Tar Baby's might be the one, but Sissy informed me that once or twice a month the two of them get together and recount the old stories. "Tar Baby thinks the story is as funny as Gene," she reflected. "Makes me wonder about you old football players!!"

Kinda' makes me wonder about us, too!

POP ME ONE

But Duby's demand upon Tar Baby may not have been as inordinate as that perpetrated upon freshmen Sam Owen and Louis Lanter in 1957 by upper-classmen Stump Powell, Bear Brown, and Mama Roberts.

During football season, cars were anathema to football players, a long standing and absolute rule established and enforced by Coach Vaught. But after the season ended athletes were allowed to bring their autos onto campus. Sam had driven his 1957 Chevrolet convertible to Ole Miss from his home in Tennessee. It figured prominently in the episode.

Stump, Bear, and Mama came by my room late one afternoon and said to Louis and me, "Freshmen, put your ROTC uniforms on – we're going to Memphis to Danny's Club."

"How're we goin'?" Sam asked.

"How in hell do you think?" one of the varsity players

answered. "In your car. Here, wear these – you're driving, chauffeur."

He handed Sam a pair of white gloves.

When the five athletes exited the athletic dorm, Stump barked to Sam, "Freshman, pull your car up beside that one right there." Then glancing around to insure the absence of Wobble, he quickly transferred four cases of beer from that car to Sam's. Bear stuck his shotgun under the seat.

"Now get the hell out of here, freshman!"

About half-way between the campus and town, Stump told Sam to pull the car over. Then turning toward Louis, he said, "Get your ass in the boot."

"The boot?" asked the freshman, "What's that?"

"The trunk, Rural. You know, where the top folds up."

"How am I gonna get in there – the top is in it, and the cover's on it."

"Not for long," Bear responded.

With that, the upper-classman pulled a knife out of his pocket and commanded, "Freshman, put the top up."

"After I put the top up," Sam recalled, "Bear snapped the cover shut over the boot hole and cut a two-foot square hole in it. Then he turned again to Louis and said, "Now Freshman, get in it."

Louis eased himself through the opening into the trunk.

"Now get over to one side," the upper-classman commanded. When Louis moved over, Bear dumped the four cases of beer into the boot. "Spread them around, Freshman."

Looking at the uniformed driver, Mama Roberts then ordered, "Driver, take us to the ice house."

"By the time we got to the ice house," Sam remembered, "Louis had wallowed himself out a place to sit midst the 96 cans of beer. Only his head stuck up through the hole."

"How much ice you figure we need, Stump," Mama asked. "A hundred pounds?"

"Naw, probably not that much. Get fifty crushed."

"Sam, wait a minute," I interrupted. "Where did Louis sit after they poured the ice in–!"

"I don't remember exactly, but I think he stacked some beer cans up and sat on them, but I know he sat against the rear of the boot and propped his feet on the front. That kept his feet dry, kind of–!"

"Did you get mad when they cut a hole in your cover?", I asked.

"Hell, Paige, don't you remember? Freshmen didn't get mad at varsity. We were more concerned about protecting our butts."

"I remember," I assured him.

"Anyway, after the beer and Louis received the ice, they told me to get on Highway 7 and head to Memphis. Every few minutes one of them would yell, 'Bartender, pop me one.' That was before flip-top cans, so they gave Louis a 'church key', and every time one of them yelled for a beer, you would see this arm stretch out of my boot with a cold one."

So with a uniformed chauffeur complete with white gloves and a uniformed bartender, the three varsity Ole Miss football players were driven to the city, where "we hit Danny's and every other night-club in Memphis and West Memphis," mused Sam. "They were feeling pretty good by the time we got to Memphis, and they got us in a fight at Danny's. By the time we left West Memphis, they were way past three sheets in the wind."

Heading South now, Stump hollered, "Freshman, take us't Clark-dale–'air's sum' nite clubs 'air in Marx an' Batesville whut we hadn't hit yet – WHOOPEE, we gonna' party in Clark-dale – let 'er eat, ye'r damn freshman, let 'er eat."

The five footballers invaded the VFW in Clarksdale, probably less than a welcome sight to the locals, most of whom looked upon college football players with some scorn.

"As soon as we walked into the building," Sam reminisced, "Bear headed straight for the bandstand where he promptly stopped the music, grabbed the microphone and announced with alcoholic diction, 'Ah want t' day'nce wif' thu' ugliest woman in heah.'

"I couldn't believe it," Sam laughed, "but several women dashed up to Bear and he danced with them all. Made their boyfriends, or husbands or whatever, mad as hell."

"Let's get out of heah," finally one of the three wisely demanded – and they did.

The intoxicated three, the chauffeur dressed in an ROTC uniform with white gloves and the bartender with a wet butt decided it was time to go home. They almost made it.

STOP HERE

"Stop th' car freshman," one of the three bellowed, "rite-cheer."

"On this bridge, sir?"

"Hell yess, on this bridge – whur'd ye thank? Stop it rite cheer. Now both o' yew, git outta' th' car."

More than reluctantly, the two freshman football players tumbled from the Chevy. The early morning Spring air was crisp. Highway 6 was deathly quiet, no other vehicle in sight. Only night sounds of rural Mississippi could be heard, an owl emitting his mournful resonance a half-mile away, a bull-frog somewhere beneath the bridge, crickets apparently awakened by the lights of the car. The smell of noxious swampy water floated up from the bog below, signifying the still deadness of the water.

Bear pulled his shotgun from under the seat of the car. Aiming straight up in the air, he fired off one loud blast, silencing the living creatures which just moments before had been sounding their clarion calls.

"Now, freshmen, jump in th' watta'," Bear commanded in his alcohol-superintended voice.

"Jump in the water," Bear repeated as he turned the shotgun slightly toward Sam. "Or had'je ruther me jist blow yer brains out?"

"Now, Paige," Sam recalled to me, "I didn't really think he'd shoot us, but we were freshmen, and we weren't absolutely sure where the upper-classman's authority stopped."

"So y'all dove in?"

"We jumped in, trying not to think about the doubtful murky distance from the bridge to the pungent water nor if we would land on stumps nor what reptiles might be waiting for us beneath the toxic water. We just jumped."

"What happened?" I quizzed.

"We fell about ten feet, landed in waist-deep rancid water and sunk up to our knees in mud on the bottom – what a mess. You should have seen us and our ROTC uniforms when we waded out–!"

The disheveled and soggy soldiers stood on the shoulder of the highway and discussed their plight as they watched the tail-lights of Sam's car disappear in the distance.

"Well, hell," Louis complained to Sam, "guess we'd better start walkin'!"

"How far were you from the campus?" I asked.

"Five or six miles. We walked into the dorm just after daylight. First thing I looked for was my car."

It sat contentedly in the parking lot by the dorm.

"Tell me the truth, Sam," I challenged him, "did you and Louis get mad at the three highwaymen?"

"Hell no," Sam exclaimed, "we stuffed it. Don't you remember how it was then? Freshmen weren't allowed to get mad at upper-classmen.

CHAPTER III

ONE REASON I HATE LSU

THE BOUNTY

"Earl," I asked, "did LSU place a bounty on me when we played y'all?" "Earl," was Earl Leggett, a former 300-pound All-American tackle at LSU and more recently, an All-Pro lineman with the Chicago Bears. He and I had played against each other in College. We were driving to Cal. Western University, San Diego, in my new Ford Thunderbird for the first New Orleans Saints training camp. It was late June, 1967. Earl had been released to New Orleans by the Bears. I was the first player to sign a Saint's football contract, attempting a comeback after a six-year sabbatical.

For years I had wondered about the rumored bounty, in part because of my physical condition following the LSU games. I never motored off the battlefield at the final gun in my own strength, making the distant journey only with the aid of a manager, or two, or three.

Gossip had augmented my suspicions, passed on to me by several of my Natchez High class mates who were students at LSU.

Earl, half asleep in the front passenger's seat of my Thunderbird, stirred slightly. His eyes remained closed. "On you AND Eagle Day, but we had to get you out of the game the first half to collect it."

"What happened if you got me out the third quarter?"

"The price went down."

"How much?"

"Hell, I don't know! I can't remember," my semi-comatose companion retorted. "A good bit."

His eyes stayed shut!

"What was the full amount?" I inquired.

"Thousand dollars. I didn't think you were worth it. Eagle maybe, but not you."

"Thanks, friend."

A FAMILY REUNION

My father, mother, younger sister and I moved from Mama Poole's house at Homochitto in Amite County to Natchez in the early summer of 1952. Natchez High School had given me a scholarship, all my Crosby High friends declared. In truth, someone did give me a good-paying summer job, five and a half days a week for $37.50, a lot of money for a 16-year-old boy in 1952.

I soon discovered Natchez' summer baseball league and immediately "signed up" to play – for the Rotary Club. My coach was Jim Gilbert.

Jim worked at Rex Sports Store. He had been a fine professional baseball player himself, working his way a respectable distance up the minor league ladder before finally retiring from the Natchez Indians of the old Cotton States League. People who saw him play insisted that had he not hurt his throwing arm, he could have played in the Major Leagues, batting more than 300 at every level. He was an excellent coach, and became a good friend.

Jim had grown up in Minden, Louisiana, an older brother in a big family. One of his younger sisters, Nell, was the same age as me, a tall, slim, dark-haired beautiful model for two large clothing stores in Shreveport. When I visited Jim's home in Natchez, I found disengaging my eyes from the several pictures of her scattered around the Gilbert living room to be very difficult.

"Sure would like to meet Nell some time, Jim," I often begged.

"You will – one of these days we'll have her over here."

It was June of 1955, three years since I first saw Nell's picture, between my sophomore and junior years at Ole Miss. I was home for the summer. I dropped in on the Gilberts. I still had not met Nell.

"Sure would like to meet Nell sometime, Jim!"

"You will."

"When?"

"How about in three weeks?"

"Three weeks? Why three weeks?" with unbridled enthusiasm, I asked.

"We're having a family reunion in Minden."

"Am I invited?"

"You're invited."

"Nell gonna be there?"

"Of course," he responded. "She still lives at home with Mama, and we're having the reunion there."

My heart raced with anticipation. Several questions popped into my head.

"You ever tell her about me, Jim?"

"Of course, for the last three years."

"What did she say?"

"Well, well, ah, well, she said she'd like to meet you."

"Did she really? Great! I really want to meet her!"

I was in deep thought and several minutes passed.

"Think she'll go out with me?"

"Well – well – oh – well – I really don't know."

"She's your sister, Jim. Surely she'll go out with me if you, well – kind of – insist."

"I don't know, Paige, Nell's pretty head strong and a lot younger than I. I was grown and gone by the time she got to high school."

"Will you try?"

"Yeah, but I can't make any promises."

"Got one more question for you, Jim. Does she know I play football for Ole Miss?"

"I TOLD her."

"When?"

"Oh, I don't remember exactly. Probably when you signed your scholarship a couple of years ago."

Saturday, family reunion time, finally arrived. The early morning sun dropped a pink glow upon the Mississippi River far below us as we motored across the bridge. The Blue Cat Club and the Pirate's Club, the only buildings left in Natchez-under-the-Hill, were match boxes below us. The flat, gumbo soil of eastern Louisiana stretched into the distance, a Cajun Delta extending almost to Minden, a town of about 5,000 people nestling in the hills of the northwestern part of the state. The highway was two lane. Saturday morning would launch the country folks into all the little Louisiana towns to sell their goods and conduct their trade, doubling the population of every hamlet. Pickup trucks would clog the road.

"How long before we get there, Jim?" I wondered out loud.

"Oh, 'bout two and a half hours, I 'spect. Maybe three if we hit traffic."

With my luck, we'll hit traffic, I thought. "That's not

bad," I responded. "That'll put us there 'bout dinner time."

The Gilbert home was lovely, a large white wood frame house on a big tree-shaded lot in the middle of town. Children, grandchildren, brothers, sisters, nieces, nephews, cousins and friends covered the grounds.

"Reminds me of the Cothren and Poole reunions," I surmised.

"Let's get the food out of the trunk," Jim's wife suggested, "before all the folks surround us, and get it on the tables."

Within a few seconds, a dozen smiling relatives encompassed us, hugging necks, shaking hands. The crowd was too large for individual introductions. I looked for Nell. I couldn't see her.

"Folks, this is our friend Paige Cothren. Y'all introduce yourselves to him."

Ten minutes later I was still shaking hands with new friends, and Nell hadn't appeared. Jim walked close by, delivering the last of the food from the trunk of the car. I grabbed him by his arm, pulling him to one side.

"Where is she?"

"Just relax, Paige, she's here somewhere. We'll find her in a minute."

I heard the screen door slam shut behind me, and I immediately recognized her. Nell smiled, walked across the elevated veranda toward us and down the seven or eight steps to the yard. She wore white shorts, a sleeveless purple top and sandals. Her dark hair cascaded down her back, and her smiling red lips revealed two rows of beautiful white teeth. Her long, tanned legs were carved brownstone and immaculately shaped, lending evidence to an athletic lifestyle, or perhaps to her profession. "Models walk a lot," I thought, "so does she model because she has beautiful legs, or does she have beautiful legs because she models – or both?"

As Nell moved across the thirty feet of freshly-cut front yard toward us, that philosophical question suddenly lost its import.

I felt myself become speechless, kind of like the time, when as a teenager, I was suddenly asked to say a blessing before a meal. Had I been forced to speak at that moment, my voice would have been at least two octaves higher.

Nell ran to Jim, threw her arms around his neck, and hugged him. "How are you, Big Brother?"

Her picture had done little justice to her.

"Fine, honey, how are you?"

"Great, now that my big brother's here."

"Hum," I wondered, "could part of that joy be because he brought me?" I was standing behind Jim and to his right. Nell still had not looked at me. I wondered if my grin looked as stupid as it felt.

"Nell," Jim introduced as he turned toward me, "this is Paige. Paige, this is Nell."

I shook her hand, which she had enthusiastically thrust toward me. "It's great meeting you at last, Nell." I hoped I exuded confidence.

Smiling at me and glancing toward her brother, the brown beauty confessed, "Jim has told me a lot about you, Paige. I'm glad to meet you."

She sounded genuine.

"He's told me a lot about you, too, Nell, though not as much as I would have liked for him to—!"

Part of the smile left her face. "Y'all were about to miss

lunch. We were kind of getting worried about you."

Several large tables were scattered about the yard, each heaped with unbelievably attractive and delicious-looking dishes. A man's voice asked for quiet. "Let's have the blessing." Thirty seconds later he concluded. – "AMEN."

"Sis," Jim implored, "why don't you take Paige over and help him get something to eat. I haven't spoken to Mama yet."

Smiling again, Nell turned toward me. "You look hungry. Follow me."

"Anywhere."

Part of the smile left her face again.

"Here's the vegetable table, as you can see, and over there is the meat table. On the other side of the meat table – there – you'll find the Cajun food table. There's the drink table and next to it is the dessert table."

"Wow, Nell, you did that beautifully," I blurted. "You ever thought about working in a restaurant?"

"Thank you! I've been in training. No, I've never really thought about working in a restaurant."

Her voice lost some of its softness. The food was delicious. With Gilbert relatives all around me, I enjoyed a sumptuous feast, sitting on the floor of the veranda, my feet dangling off the edge. Nell ate in the swing.

WHERE DO YOU PLAY?

"Where do you play football, Paige? Jim told me you played."

The afternoon had passed all too quickly. I had met all the relatives and friends, most of whom had left. Only Jim's immediate family remained, his brother, his sisters, and their

49

children, about twenty people in all. The adults sat in lawn chairs beneath the giant oak trees, and the children's playful laughter drifted from the large back yard. The sun was setting, and its brilliant glow splashed against Nell's face, disclosing a magnificent silhouette. A slight afternoon breeze vibrated the leaves on the mammoth oak trees, trying in vain to cool our tepid bodies. Other than an occasional trip inside to the bathroom, I had remained outside all afternoon. Throwing a football with the young boys had warmed me even more, and anyway, it was probably wasted, I thought. Nell never seemed to notice.

I was sitting in a lawn chair beside her. She turned her head slightly toward me and into the sun, causing her to narrow her eyes.

"Where?"

"I play at Ole Miss – The University of Mississippi – you know – the Rebels."

"Oh, you do?"

Her unimpressed surprise sounded genuine!!

"Yep," I replied, trying desperately to control my excitement. "I play fullback on offense and outside linebacker on defense."

"That's nice. I saw the LSU-Ole Miss game last fall. I don't remember you."

"Nice? Don't remember me?" I thought. "How could she sit through an entire football game and not remember a starting fullback! After all, I played forty minutes, at least." I measured my response.

"I bet one reason you don't remember me is because that special boyfriend probably distracted you."

She smiled. "That could be, but another reason is that

I don't know THAT much about college football, and not knowing you, I wasn't listening for your name. Besides, how do you know a boyfriend took me?"

"Just a guess. Baton Rouge is a long way from Minden. I can't see you traveling that distance to see a college football game alone – or with the girls."

Tilting her head back, Nell laughed. Then she looked me directly in the eye, the bright setting summer sun propelling its brilliant rays through the gently shifting oak leaves, causing her to squint again.

"You're right about that, Paige. I would never have gone to Baton Rouge at night alone or with the girls. I went with my fellow."

"Sounds pretty serious."

"It is," she somberly confessed. I could hear the commitment to him in the tone and volume of her voice.

I gambled but I wanted to know. "Are you engaged?"

"Not yet. We've talked about it."

"Would you go out with me?"

Her answer was immediate and much too sharp. "No!"

I don't think I was prepared for that quick negative retort, such a sudden fervent rejection. I must have looked shocked. I felt a rare heat rush from somewhere to the flushing surface of my embarrassed face.

Her voice softened. "Paige, even if he and I weren't serious about our relationship, I still probably wouldn't date you," the brown beauty explained. "We're too different. I've always dated – well – the other kind, especially these last few years."

I could tell the conversation was beginning to discomfort Nell. Her voice was gentle, her face soft, but I wasn't about to punt – not on third down.

"What other kind?"

"Well," she hesitated, "I really don't want to talk about it. I don't want to say anything unkind—!"

After two years under the Ole Miss coaching staff, especially Wobble, I figured my feelings lay beyond the damaging ability of a young woman, even an extremely beautiful one. I ignored my blushing face.

"Come on, Nell, tell me. You can't hurt my feelings."

"Well, o.k., but I really don't want to say it —."

"What kind?" I looked her directly in the eyes. She paused twenty seconds, thinking.

"The more intellectual kind? The student-businessman kind?"

Asking the answer rather than declaring it intended to lessen its harm, I think. I tore my eyes away from hers and turned my head. Mother was right – I should be studying.

"See, I knew it would hurt you," Nell quickly affirmed. "I shouldn't have said it."

I think my face grew redder. "You didn't hurt my feelings," I avowed. "I don't get my feelings hurt! Will you write to me if I write you?"

I was looking at her again. It was fourth down, but I still refused to punt. Besides, a sympathetic heart often violates self-imposed restrictions.

Nell said nothing, her body rigid.

"Will you?"

She shifted slightly in her chair.

"Will you?"

The beauty turned again toward me. The sun had dropped out of sight, the wind had died, granting rest to the oak leaves. For ten seconds she paused.

"I'll write you as a friend ONLY, o.k.?"

"O.K."

Necks were hugged, Nell had shaken my hand again, and the sky was completely dark when the three of us headed back toward Natchez.

"It was a great day, Jim. Thank you both for inviting me. I had a good time, and I love your family. By the way, the pictures failed to do Nell justice."

"She is pretty," Mrs. Gilbert concurred, "Isn't she?"

"I would use a stronger word than 'pretty'. Even beautiful might fall short."

"How did it go with her, Paige?" Jim asked. "Looked like the two of you were doing a lot of talking."

"It could have been worse. She won't date me, but she agreed to write. I'll work from there."

Both laughed. I could not tell if they were laughing at me or with me. I didn't ask.

THE SUMMER

Throughout the remainder of July and August, Nell and I wrote once every ten days or so. My letters were warm, romantic, and suggestive. Hers were formal, cool, and friendly. She occasionally mentioned her boyfriend and what they were doing. In defense of my pride and vindication of my ego, I wrote about all the beautiful Natchez girls whom I dated. From the contents of her letters, I determined that I was affected more by what she was doing than was she by my activities. Her comments seemed to be congratulatory.

I wanted jealousy, not congratulations!

Anyway, the summer finally passed and August 30, the reporting date for Ole Miss varsity football players, arrived. On that day we were given our physicals. The following day we received our equipment, and on September 1 we started two-a-day practices. We opened the 1955 football season against Georgia on September 17, with only two short weeks to prepare.

THE SEASON

September 17, 1955, I made college football history, as insignificant as the event sounds today. I kicked two field goals in our 26 to 13 win. Those two field goals tied the national collegiate record for most field goals in one game; they set an SEC record for most field goals kicked in one game; and they set an Ole Miss record for the most field goals kicked in a season. Even more importantly to my ego, however, they made headlines of almost every sports page in America, so rare was the feat.

Tuesday, September 20, I excitedly unsealed a letter from Nell. In it she expressed surprise and pleasure at opening the Shreveport newspaper Sunday morning and seeing my name emblazoned across the top of the sports page – Ole Miss' Cothren Kicks Two Field Goals.

I think my pleasure at Nell's discovery surpassed hers. "Man," I thought, "field goals contain all kinds of hidden value."

After a controversial loss to Kentucky September 24, Ole Miss embarked upon a fourteen game winning streak stretching into the 1956 season. By the middle of October, I had received many letters from the Minden beauty – with articles clipped from the sports pages. I enjoyed reading about me that which I knew she had read. My anticipation grew when she mentioned coming to the LSU game, not to mention my ego!

Then we played Arkansas in Oxford, our Homecoming game. The Razorbacks confidently rode into town undefeated, anchored in the line by their All-American tackle, Billy Ray Smith, later to become my friend and teammate with the L.A. Rams.

We won 17-7, and I was selected National Back of the Week. My picture appeared on the sports page of practically every major newspaper in America.

"Um-hunh," I arrogantly asserted to my roomie Jerry McKaskel, "Betcha' Nell is gonna see THAT!"

He shook his head in disgust.

I received a letter from Nell every day the following week. They were warm, romantic, suggestive. In one of them she announced that she had broken up with her boyfriend and that she and a girlfriend wanted to come to the LSU game in Baton Rouge. "Could I get her two tickets," she asked, "and could I get her friend a date with an Ole Miss football player?"

"Of course," I wrote, "if your friend is pretty and fun."

We formulated plans – on the phone.

At last I would have my date with Nell!

I couldn't wait!

But I had to wait – though only a week. We had played Arkansas October 22. We would play LSU October 29.

I sent Nell the two tickets and informed her I had gotten her friend a date. I told her where we would get off the bus at the stadium, and where we planned to go after the game – the La Louisianne Club. "Nell," I wrote, "we probably won't have more than two hours. We usually have bed check even after games." I also warned her that I could do nothing more than speak to her when we got off the bus. The coaches demanded a "game-face." "I guarantee you, Nell, that I would lose mine if given a few minutes to greet you. Be right outside our dressing room after the game," I instructed.

* * * * *

I saw her immediately upon exiting the bus, standing next to her very attractive friend, in front of a large contingent of Ole Miss supporters. She was dressed in Red and Blue, a Rebel flag in one hand, waving vigorously with the other.

I smiled, looked at Buster, said "hi" and walked right on by. I hoped she understood. I sensed adoring eyes follow me to the dressing room, but it may have only been my over-active imagination. I glanced back toward her before entering the building. I couldn't see her. I saw Buster looking at me.

"Keep your mind on the game," my uncle growled.

I silently wondered how.

THE GAME

We beat LSU that night on the scoreboard 29 to 26, but I think they might have outscored us physically. I'm not completely certain, because I don't remember much of the game due partly to the passage of time but primarily to my battered brain. I DO know that they scored four touchdowns and two extra points. We scored three touchdowns, three extra points, a safety, and I kicked two field goals. Their two leading players were O.K. Ferguson, a big, bruising fullback from Woodville, Mississippi, with whom I had played summer baseball before moving to Natchez, and Leggett. And I remember vividly what happened to me.

By the end of the first quarter, the purple Tigers had

purpled my right eye and closed it. By the half, both lips were "busted," swollen, protruding straight out, and draining something which looked like Blush Zinfandel Wine, though it certainly tasted differently. By the end of the third quarter, a carefully planted elbow or fist introduced my nose to my cheekbone. Eagle Day, our quarterback, inserted his two forefingers up my two nostrils and straightened it. "Looks pretty straight, Paige." I could still, however, see out of my left eye – that is – until the fourth quarter.

I played left outside linebacker on defense, a position similar to corner back in today's defensive schemes. My responsibilities included "containing" on running plays and covering the flat on passes.

With about five minutes left in the close and bruising contest, Ferguson ran a fullback sweep toward me. I trailed him to the sideline, timing my arrival there to the moment he turned up field. Buster would approve – I had O.K. hemmed in –! At the same second I dropped my shoulder to make the tackle, an 18-wheeler threw his enlarged torso into the back of my weary legs, a clip. My knees collapsed forward and my body twisted backward. Ferguson, turned up-field by the sideline at that instant, pumped his right knee into my unprotected left eye, finding the only unabused spot on my maltreated face. The lights in Tiger Stadium suddenly intensified and immediately disappeared.

I regained a degree of consciousness somewhere between the point of assault and the Ole Miss bench, on my feet in a manner of speaking, a student manager attached to each arm. I knew I wasn't in Heaven because my preacher promised Heaven contains no pain. I wasn't sure about hell. The only thing I DID know was how much I DIDN'T know: where I was, what I was doing there, where I was being dragged, and who was dragging me – against my stuporous will. I wanted to lie down but my two man handlers wouldn't let me.

"Just a little farther, Paige," I heard one of them say. He was yelling out of a well.

"Oh, I'm Paige?"

"Yes, you're Paige and we're almost to the bench."

"What bench?"

"The Ole Miss bench."

"Oh!" I knew Ole Miss. All my Poole relatives had played football there.

The two wrestlers eased me onto the bench.

"I wanta' lie down," I pleaded.

"O.K.," someone said out of the well, as the two lowered me to the cool ground.

"Wow, now he's lost his left eye," I heard someone declare way off.

"I lost my left eye?"

"No, no, I didn't mean you LOST it, I just meant that it's closed – like the right one."

"Is that why I can't see?"

"Probably! – look at that nose!"

"What's wrong with my nose?"

"It's broken again, but we can fix it."

I felt two objects slide into my nostrils and then a sharp pain supported by a familiar crunching sound.

"There, that looks pretty good."

"What about my teeth?"

"You still got THEM – 'course you remember you had two broken off against Kentucky."

"Against Kentucky?"

About then I smelled a sharp, pungent odor. I tried to turn my swollen head, but I couldn't – it was lodged between two immovable objects.

"WHAT'S THAT?", I heard myself yell.

"Smelling salts! Don't you recognize it?"

"It's over, Paige, WE BEAT 'EM," someone cried. "WE BEAT 'EM!"

"Who?"

"LSU – We beat 'em!"

I remember thinking that must be good, beating LSU.

"Can you walk into the dressing room, Paige?" someone asked.

"I guess so, but I can't see much."

"We'll lead you."

By the time I had, with the aid of my two guides, undressed, showered, and re-dressed in my street clothes, I had regained almost total consciousness, a fact proven by the severe pain.

I was seated on a bench putting my shoes on when her name exploded in my pugilistic brain.

"NELL!! What am I going to do about Nell?"

"Richard, how do I look?", I quickly asked.

I had recognized Richard Weiss' voice. He was one of our starting tackles, and he occupied the locker next to mine.

"Not too good, Unca' Bus, your face is – well – kind of a mess."

"Really looks bad, huh?"

"Bad? – Bad?" I heard one of my eavesdropping, compassionate compatriots exclaim. "Bad? Ha, Ha, Ha, Ha! Bad – you ever see the South end of a North bound mule?"

"With his tail raised," another taunting teammate yelled.

Laughter filled the dressing room.

"It does look kinda' bad," Richard repeated.

"What worries me is that I can't see!"

"Man, if Nell is as good-looking as you say she is, I'd be worried about those ruptured lips draining that gook!", someone hollered from across the room.

"I am," I answered, "but she probably won't want to be seen with me, though."

"I don't know," another teammate quipped, "I think it's an improvement."

"QUIET, MEN!"

It was Coach Vaught. I remember little of what he said except his final, glorious words.

"Fellows, tough game tonight but we won, so we're going to give you the night out – NO BED-CHECK."

The collective roar of fifty exhilarated football players was deafening.

"Hello, La Louisiane Club," a loud voice exclaimed.

"Hello, morning light," another echoed.

I turned toward the place where I last heard Richard's voice. "I finally got a date with a beautiful girl after three years of trying, no bed-check, and now this –!!"

"We'll meet at La Louisiane, fellows," Eddie Crawford, a halfback announced. "See you there."

"See you at La Louisiane?" I sneered. "Hell, I can't even see how to get out of this stupid dressing room."

But I could partially see. I had discovered while dressing that I could push the swelling above my left eye up with my left forefinger; the lower swelling down with my left thumb, and partially see. Assuming that posture, I followed the crowd to the dressing room door and through it. Hundreds of Rebel fans were gathered immediately outside, and I felt the cool late October air at the same moment I heard their cheers. I wondered if Nell would be difficult to find.

I pushed the swelling harder.

"Is that Cothren?" someone yelled.

"Can't tell," a voice answered.

With a face like mine, who COULD tell, I thought.

I was searching the excited crowd through my one bloody, swollen, and teary eye when I felt a small, warm hand slip into my right one. Then I heard her voice, soft, compassionate, caring, concerned – the question indicating uncertainty. "Paige?"

"Nell!" I quickly turned my head so I could see her with my left eye. She moved to my front.

"Great game, Paige," she whispered.

"Thank you. I paid for it."

"You sure did."

"Great game means a lot coming from an LSU fan."

"An ex-LSU fan," she replied as she raised her Rebel flag and waved it to the cheering crowd, many of whom had been watching.

"You sure you want to be seen with this mess?"

"I'm sure! I came a long way–!"

"I promised a couple of other players and their dates a ride – that o.k.?"

"The more the merrier," mused Nell. "My car will hold eight if the girls will sit on some laps."

"I don't think the guys will mind. You'll have to drive though. I can't see."

DANCING IN THE DARK

Weiss yelled at me as the eight of us groped our way into the night club. "Hell, Paige, doesn't matter if you can't see. It's dark in here. I have two good eyes, and I can't see."

We danced all night, or tried to–! My mutilated head kept spinning and throbbing. I was forced to sit many of the dances out and was far less than my usual partying self. About 4:00 or 4:30 a.m., someone announced, "Fellows we'd better get back to the motel. The bus pulls out at 7:00 for the airport. Let's go!"

Nell drove us back to the motel, where two players and their dates got out of the car. She and I sat in the front seat. Her friend and the other player sat in the back. Taking Nell's hand, I said, "Thank you for coming. I've been looking forward to this night for a long time. Sorry I look so bad – guess those Cajun boys didn't like me dating one of their ladies."

I think the beauty smiled. I really couldn't see her too well even pushing the swelling back.

"Where are you going when you leave here?" I inquired.

"I have a girlfriend here in Baton Rouge who said we could sleep at her place before heading home."

"I never had a date with a beauty whom I couldn't even see. Now I know the meaning of the song "Dancing in the Dark.""

"It was nice, Paige, knowing you were out with me and

couldn't even see 'what' some people think is pretty. I know you were very uncomfortable. Are you alright?"

"I think so. I'll know in a day or two! We need to go, I guess," I reluctantly asserted. "I don't want to–!" I opened the car door.

"Nell, I'd love to kiss you, but I wouldn't expect anyone to touch these ludicrous lips."

Nell leaned over toward me and bussed my right cheek. "About the only undamaged spot on your head," she softly said.

"It's the only place which isn't sore. We gonna' keep writing?"

"I don't know, Paige."

"What do you mean you don't know?"

She hesitated – much too long. "I don't know."

"Will you think about it?"

"I'll think about it," she replied softly, reflectively. "I'll think about it."

Nell's car disappeared toward town, as the sun's first amber glow eased into the shadowy Eastern horizon, reminding me of thick Louisiana molasses spreading across a grey plate. I stood there for a long time wondering what had happened, unable even to remember much about the night. Finally, I felt my way into the depressive motel room, packed my clothes and shaving items and with the aid of my roommate, made my way to the restaurant.

"My," the waitress asked, "What happened to you?"

"I think I made a bunch of Cajuns mad."

"Like anything to eat?"

"No, I'm kinda' sick at my stomach. Just bring me some

coffee."

* * * * *

Earl Leggett rolled the windows down and stuck four fingers out. "Damn hot out there. Reckon it's gonna be like this in San Diego?"

"I don't know, Earl, but it's the last of June. It's supposed to be hot. You in shape?"

"Haven't run a step. Training Camp's gonna kill me."

I had finished telling the huge tackle the saga of Nell. Like my "consoling" Ole Miss teammates, he thought the whole thing was funny.

"I remember them taking you off the field, Paige. I saw your face. Ug. – man, no self-respecting woman could have stomached being seen with THAT!"

"Thanks a lot, Big-un, your sympathy overwhelms me."

My "compassionate" companion then reclined his seat again back as far as it would go, folded his arms behind his indifferent head and reflected, "You know it WAS kind of barbaric, putting a bounty on you. Couldn't get by with it today. Your face was a bloody mess, and I say that as an American, not an Englishman – that air as cold as it will go?"

I turned the air conditioner temperature down.

"I'm not sure you qualify as an American, Leggett – Americans exhibit some feelings, and pity, and sympathy."

"Hey man, I have feelings. I feel like hell that I didn't collect that bounty!"

"You just said the bounty was barbaric."

"Had a weak moment. It passed!"

"To be honest," I admitted, "I would have put YOU out of the game if I could have. In fact, I tried."

"What happened?"

"That's when I got my first black eye."

"Good. I can understand why you'd be a little p–sed at us though, what with the pain, blood, swelling, and all that. You think that's why your face looks like it does today?"

"Man, I don't care about a little pain and blood, and I'm kind of proud of the bounty."

"What then?"

"Nell! I spent three years working her up to that date, then not only did I look like hell, but I couldn't even see her – or kiss her. No one can propagate a romance if he can't even kiss the girl."

"Propagate! Propagate! Where in hell did you learn such a big word – 'propagate'?"

"Not in Tiger Stadium," I asserted.

"You learn ANYTHING in Tiger Stadium?"

"Yeah, I learned not to date a girl after a bounty has been placed on me."

"Glad to help fine-tune your education," the Saints tackle concluded. "Serves you right for trying to steal one of our beautiful girls."

For ten minutes or so, I was lost in deep, contemplative thought. When I glanced over at the huge lineman, he was sound asleep. A minute later he was snoring.

POSTSCRIPT

When our pilot dropped the plane down for us to see the Ole Miss campus from the air on the trip home, I lost consciousness. I was taken to a hospital upon landing in Memphis, where I spent the night. A doctor revived me.

I practiced Monday through Friday and played the following Saturday.

Nell and I began dating again and continued for about six months until both of us started dating others. I haven't seen her or talked to her in 43 years, at this writing.

Earl Leggett has for many years coached various teams in the National Football League.

I continue to exult in hating LSU.

CHAPTER IV

OFF THE FIELD

INTRODUCTION

Until my senior year, I attended Crosby High School in Amite County. Crosby was then and still is a small sawmill town. In the 40's it bustled with business spawned by World War II and the population of about 1,000 was evenly divided between black and white. The mill, owned by Mr. H. H. Crosby, from whom the town drew its name, radiated out over 100 acres in the middle of the minuscule village. Every home and every business, admittedly few in number, was owned by Mr. Crosby. Everything, therefore, in the town belonged to him and everyone worked for him, including the 100 or so men who drove the 100 or so log trucks which for years ran day and night.

The school system in Crosby, although registered as a public school, operated more like a private one, controlled by the man for whom the town was named. He hired and he fired the teachers and he superintended the school superintendent, with a firm, uncompromising fist. Mr. Crosby demanded and acquired an excellent high school. As students we toed the line with a smile on our faces. Remember those days?

Mr. Crosby also wanted a competitive athletic program at dear ol' Crosby High so he hired a man, deceased now, whom I believe to be one of the greatest coaches ever to prowl any side-line, Hugh Bowlen. Cud'n Hugh, as we affectionately called him, had married a local girl, who was related to many of us, hence his name, Cud'n.

Cud'n Hugh enticed almost every boy in the high school of less than 100 students to come out for football and in 1949, employing a "short-punt" offensive formation, similar to the Notre Dame Box, we won the State Class B Championship with an 11-0 record. I was 14 years old, in the ninth grade, the starting right guard, and scared to death.

> "Julius Caesar Cicero dear
> We're the team that has no fear
> We're not rough and we're not tough
> We're 'dis Crosby strutting our stuff!!"

Now, admit it! Motivated by heart-rending, emotion-creating, blood-stirring yells like that, wouldn't you give your all for dear old Alma Mater?

Anyway, Crosby became known in Mississippi for winning a state football championship but it won athletic acclaim for another reason too. In a twenty year period, that small high school, tucked away in the rolling, pine covered hills of the southwest corner of the state, delivered 13 football players on scholarship to Ole Miss; ten Pooles or Poole relatives; Cloyce and Charles Hinton; and Jack Cavin. Several other alumni toiled at smaller colleges.

From the rural countryside and Crosby, Ole Miss invited a cousin, Jimmy Carol Robertson, whose mother is a Poole, and me to visit and view the 1951 Spring game. I was a sophomore at Crosby High. We spent the night before the game in Crawford Mims' room.

Crawford made All-American playing guard for Ole Miss and he was one of my heroes. I was enraptured for an entire weekend, fascinated by Ole Miss itself, the players, and the Coaches.

The trance continued two years later when I moved into Garland Hall permanently for four years, but in part for a different reason. Wobble Davidson was our dorm parent. On page 17 of *Walk Carefully Around the Dead*, I explained.

Wobble and Sara and their children lived in an apartment on the northeast corner of the first floor of Garland Dorm. He was our vicarious parent, our Mom and Dad all rolled up into one. He possessed the perfect attributes for a task-master: sharp eye-sight, acute hearing, flawless sense of smell, quick mind, strong stair-climbing legs, the ability to impute fear into the toughest athlete, and a great sense of humor. Wobble would punish us severely one day and do it in such a way that we would find it humorous the next day–.

For a country boy, matriculating from high school via Natchez, Garland Hall was a fascinating place. It housed my football heroes and it offered running water and indoor toilets, both of which came to Mama Poole's years after I had gone.

It also featured Wobble, who because of his characteristics tuned and refined our senses of hearing. Before enrolling at Ole Miss I could hear a squirrel gnaw a hickory nut at 100 yards. After 4 years of listening for Wobble, I could hear the same sound at a quarter of a mile.

WHAT PRICE COOL AIR?

Few discomforts remain more firmly lodged upon the memory of Ole Miss Rebel football players than the temperature inside the athletic dorm before the miracle of conditioned air. Misery gained perfection by practicing in 95 degree heat; shuffling to the smothering athletic cafeteria afterwards in 90 degrees; and trying to sleep in an 85 degree oven called Garland, which was always 5 degrees warmer than the temperature outside, even at 3:00 a.m. The single windows (except in corner rooms) were peep-holes splashed against a kiln wall with twist-open handles, designed to allow, for some mystic reason, only one lung-full of air into the room at a time. Fights sometimes occurred between team-mates, struggling to capture the bed nearest the miniature fissure.

We never stopped sweating. We sweated on the field, on the walk to the cafeteria, and then in the dorm. We never slept much either. Sometimes during the hottest nights, we would quietly drag our mattresses onto the grass outside the dorm for a few minutes of 5 degree-less rest. Wobble's inspection tours would send us scrambling fearfully back inside.

The Lyric and Ritz Theaters afforded athletes the only two places in Oxford where we might cool our thermal bodies for awhile, if we owned thirty-five cents. Never mind the probability that we had already seen the movies back in our hometowns, especially during two-a-day practice, before school started. We sought comfort, not entertainment, and we always left vacant seats between us, which helped us refrigerate faster. The mile walk back to Garland though, always reactivated the salty condensation, and by the time we reached home, we were hot again.

Few of us could afford fans. Those who could were viewed as wealthy. They were also highly desired as room-mates, almost as much as a corner room. The fans wouldn't cool the air, but they did move it, which made it feel better.

In 1955, Johnny Williams and Tar-Baby Bowman roomed together. The heat of two-a-days and everything else convinced them to buy a fan regardless of the cost. They pooled their assets.

"This is the latest thing in fans," the hardware salesman exhorted, "a water-cooled window fan."

"What do you mean, water-cooled?" Tar-Baby asked. "How does it work?"

"You see these little tubes?"

"Yes."

"Well," the salesman explained, "you fill them up with water and when the fan blows the air across them, they cool it some."

"How much?"

"A good bit. You can feel the difference."

Turning toward his roomie, Tar-Baby asked, "Can we afford it?"

"Gonna take all our money, but what th' hell! We'll be cool."

* * * * *

"You know what, Johnny? That air is cooler!"

The two proud "engineers" stood before their humming purchase, mounted in the window, smiles of satisfaction smeared across their perspiring faces.

"But the air's not going to hit my bed!" Gayle complained.

"It's not gonna' hit mine very good either."

"What if we moved both beds together in the middle of the room? We could put the desk and our chest-of-drawers up against the wall. That'd work," reasoned Tar-Baby.

Johnny agreed. "Might as well try it."

"I had been dating a lot," Gayle explained, "and I was really involved with my girlfriend back in Pascagoula. By the time we bought and installed the fan, I hadn't seen her in a week and I really missed her – I guess TOO much."

Sometime during the night Tar-Baby dreamed about his girlfriend. His deep and pleasant sleep was shattered by his roomie's yells. "Get off of me, you little T–d! Wake up – wake up!"

"I woke up," the little halfback recalled, "with my arms around Johnny, trying to get up on him."

That ended their comradeship of repose.

"Damn the cool air," Johnny fumed, as he pushed his bed back against the wall.

THE SWEETNESS OF SLEEP

I sympathize with light sleepers. I am one! I have a hard time sleeping when bombarded with unusual noises, especially inconstant ones. I might eventually adjust to the rhythm of a leaky faucet if the drips are invariant. If not, they become nuggets of unwelcome noise which forces my inert brain into consciousness. So I understand the plight of Happy Jack Odom, a starting end for Ole Miss in the late Forties.

Jack, Tom (Tip-Toe) Hardy and Chubby Ellis were rooming together in Vardaman Hall. The two starting guards, Bob Fuerst and Jimmy Crawford, roomed next to them.

Unlike Happy Jack, Fuerst and Crawford were very sound sleepers, dropping into the sweet bliss almost every night with their radio playing. When the station went off the air at mid-night, the radio emitted a shrill buzzing sound until a teammate, often Jack, now awakened and infuriated by the sound, turned it off. After a few months, he demanded satisfaction!

Jack's retaliation sometimes consisted of spinning a weight on the concrete floor of his next door neighbor's room, often at 3:00 a.m., an act which not only propelled Fuerst and Crawford from their beds, but awakened every person in the dorm. The spinning weight sent its ominous sound wavering through the concrete floor into the steel frame, and throughout the building. As the weight slowed, it turned over on its side and spun faster and faster, leading awakening sleepers to believe it would never end.

"By the time it stopped," Chubby recalled, "every football player in the dorm was wide awake, mad, and threatening to kill Odom."

"If you don't want me spinning the weights," Jack asserted, "then make those idiots next door turn their radio off."

One night, Jack spun his infamous noise-maker and quickly went back to bed, a bed which rested upon several months of collective trash.

"Jack never cleaned under his bed," declared Chubby. "In fact, he stored newspapers and old clothes under there. It was a mess. Well, after Jack had waked up everybody in the dorm with his spinning weight, he finally went to sleep."

Will Glover, a halfback, had not gone back to sleep though, and he wanted revenge.

"It was close to Christmas," continued Chubby, "and Will had bought several of those long firecrackers, which we called chasers. He lit one and threw it into our room."

The chaser ricocheted off all four walls, slid across the desk in the middle of the room and skidded under Odom's bed where it exploded – and set the garbage dump on fire.

"The explosion rocked Jack's bed," laughed Chubby, whom Odom called Horse, "and fire was shooting up all under his mattress and around the bed."

"Jack, Jack, get up – get out of there," Ellis cried. "You're gonna burn up!"

The roasted roomie finally leaped from his fiery resting place, scattered the burning debris and stomped out the flames. Then turning his sooty face and watery eyes toward

Chubby he exclaimed with measured apprehension, "Damn, Horse, I thought there for a minute I was already in hell!"

YOU DID WHAT IN MY BED

Football players at Ole Miss in the late forties, fifties and early sixties enjoyed a camaraderie unlike any that I've ever experienced anywhere or anytime. We tried to kill each other on the practice field and aggravate each other to death in the dorm, yet seldom did we lose our tempers with one another. We clung together like a fraternity in a time when the coaches refused to allow us to join a real fraternity. Nighttime would often find us gathered together in the grill or lined up on four or five rows at one of the two theaters in town, with seats left vacant between us, of course. The requirements of comradeship halted short of having to sit next to each other at a movie, no matter how crowded the building.

Rooster Aiken, a small running back in the late fifties, had his friendship with his roomie tested. A fastidious dresser, on ROTC drill days, he would display his uniform on his made-up bed before he left for class in the morning.

"He did that," one of his teammates declared, "because he had little time between his last class and drill time; so he would get his uniform ready, laying his neatly ironed shirt next to his crisply ironed khaki trousers with all his impeccable brass perfectly shined. Then he placed his exquisitely shined black shoes with military socks on the floor directly beneath his pants."

When I was told this story, I marveled as much about a football player who made his bed each morning as I did about one who was so committed to appearing neat on the drill field.

Almost every drill day, though, the meticulous half-back's roommate tried to destroy the effort of the conscientious soldier. At some point in the day the reprobate roomie would paint Rooster's resplendent black shoes white. Having no time to expunge the white and replace the black, he became the only Army ROTC cadet in Ole Miss history to march in glowing white shoes, to his chagrin and the dismay of his superiors.

His demerits mounted.

When finally Rooster convinced his military authorities that he could not reverse his roommate's dastardly painting prank, he was granted immunity. Roomie, having then lost the power of his persecution, devised another form of molestation.

Rooster had worked his way through the cafeteria lunch line one day, found a seat and was about to enjoy his first bite when his roommate stopped across the table directly in front of him. A fork full of food in his right hand, Rooster looked up into his roomie's roguish eyes. No one at the table spoke as they waited for Roomie's assertion, certain that one was forthcoming.

"Rooster," the renegade roommate casually declared, "I s–t in your bed."

In concerned disbelief, the diminutive halfback dropped his fork of food onto his plate and waited for Roomie to laugh, to say he was only kidding. A minute of convincing silence forced him to wonder!

Vaulting from his chair, the shifty running back sprinted to his room, hoping against hope that his roommate was only joking. Thrusting his key into the lock, Rooster threw open the door and discovered an unconscionable truth–!

He wasn't kidding!

What price friendship? Certainly for most of us, far short of that–!!

LIKE THE WAY THEY TASTE, HUH?

At this writing, I haven't smoked a cigarette, nor a pipe, nor a Hav-a-Tampa-Jewel with a wooden tip in 27 years. Wait, let me correct that – I did try a Hav-a-Tampa-Jewel with a wooden tip about 3 years ago, but I didn't inhale. The smoke kept burning my throat.

I feel a little sorry for people who smoke – oh, not because it's unhealthy, according to the medical community. My sympathy flows from the fact that we non-smokers have devised and effected a plan to push them outside, which kinda makes them second class citizens. They look so hurt when forced to congregate under the sun or stars to enjoy their favorite pastime, especially on hot days, or extremely cold ones.

I don't have the answer and I know most people demand a smoke-free environment, understandably, a cultural trend just now catching on. However, football players at Ole Miss in the forties, fifties, and early sixties lived in a relatively smoke-free environment before it became fashionable, created not by the Doctors of Medicine but by the Doctor of Discipline, Wobble Davidson. The majority of us learned to "just say no" long ago, not to preserve our lungs but to protect our entire bodies from the "omni-present" annihilator of nicotine.

No one loves anything or anybody more than a committed smoker likes cigarettes. I once confessed to my Dad, who for 65 years smoked from one to three packs of cigarettes a day depending upon whether or not he was quitting, that I wished I could love anything – another person, football, a beating, poison – anything – as much as he loved tobacco. He didn't reply. He didn't quit smoking either.

Anyway, one day several football players decided to light up in Garland Dorm: Kent Lovelace, Gayle (Tar-Baby) Bowman, and two others. Within a few minutes the closed room was filled with cigarette smoke. The portentous puffers soon remembered how the "hound of dissipation" like a beagle tracking a rabbit, could follow smoke to its sordid source. Tar-Baby decided to check the hallway. Very quietly the vigilant halfback, with his left hand, turned the doorknob and eased the door open, his right hand supporting the weight of his body against the door-frame. With cigarette in mouth, he ever so slowly peered around the corner – right into the chest of the freshman coach, who, with arms and legs crossed, rested against the hall wall. Tar-Baby froze, his body stiffening, his legs becoming Jell-O. He slowly raised his reluctant eyes to meet Wobble's, the cigarette smoke enveloping the placid coach's face. Finally, Tar-Baby's eyes met his mentor's.

"Kind of like the way they taste, huh, Tar-Baby—?"

When the other three transgressors heard the sound of the coach's voice, they crushed their cigarettes in their hands, rammed them into their pants-pockets, quickly opened the room window and began fanning the suspended smoke, hanging over the room like a big cumulus cloud, out the opening.

"—Well, why don't you just eat that cigarette?"

"Eat it?"

"Chew it – and swallow it!"

With that the slender athlete sucked the cigarette into his mouth, chewed for a couple of seconds and swallowed.

Wobble turned and walked down the hall. Tar-Baby's companions, relieved of one problem, quickly checked their pants-pockets to avoid another one.

THE NAVY?

Several stories have been written, both in this book and *Walk Carefully Around the Dead*, about Wobble's tendency to punish Ole Miss football players by making them run vertical laps in Hemingway Stadium. Little has been discussed about the affects of those laps upon the body, especially the legs. After about 5 or 6 laps, the muscle behind the thigh cramps every time it is lifted. When the muscle cramps, the running deteriorates to a walk, then to a crawl, then to nothing – very quickly. That abatement always extracted threats from the Coach – "Get off your ass and get to running. We'll be here all night," which in turn begat various thoughts in the minds of the afflicted. Notice – I said "thoughts," not comments.

Late one afternoon in the fall of 1954, freshmen Jackie Simpson, Gayle (Tar-Baby) Bowman, and Junior Harvey were in Vardaman, the freshman football dormitory, smoking, they thought, secretly.

"We were over there smoking, blowing the smoke out the window of the room which was on the second floor of the dorm," Gayle recalls. "We didn't know Wobble was anywhere around."

Understandable! The freshmen had not yet learned that Wobble could smell cigarette smoke from his apartment in Garland Hall, across the street. They soon would!

"I think Coach Wobble must have seen the smoke coming out the window," Gayle continued. "Wasn't long after we started smoking that someone started banging on our door. We didn't know who it was, so we didn't answer it."

"Open the damn door," a gruff voice yelled.

"Hell, it's Coach Wobble," one of the puffers exclaimed.

The three culprits quickly threw their cigarette out the window. "We gotta get rid of this smoke, too!" one of them whispered, so they picked up notebooks and started fanning. Unable to rid the room of all the smoke, however, they reluctantly and fearfully opened the door.

"There stood the devil himself," Gayle exclaimed. "Coach Wobble. We knew we were caught."

"You boys smoking?" asked the Coach.

"No, Sir!" all three lied.

"Well, that's good. Meet me in the stadium after practice tomorrow."

Football practice ended at dark. Gayle, Jackie, and Junior reported to Coach Davidson in the stadium.

"Don't take off your cleats," Wobble commanded. "I'll be right here listening."

Anytime the sound of cleat against concrete stopped, Wobble blew his coach's whistle, to let the punished ones know he was still there–!

"We had run 5 or 6 laps," Gayle speculated, "and our legs were really cramping – and it was pitch-black dark. I was almost to the top of the stadium when I realized I hadn't heard Simpson's cleats in the last few seconds."

"Tar-Baby," someone whispered, "Is that you?"

Tar-Baby squinted in the dark to find the source of the sound. He figured it was Jackie.

"He was lying under a bench, a seat, at the top of the stadium as far away from Coach Wobble as he could get," reflected Tar-Baby. "I leaned over and looked down into his closed eyes, which I could barely see."

"Tar-Baby," the collapsed and despondent guard wheezed, "Let's join the damn Navy!"

I BELIEVE I GOT IT!

For many years now, football players have borne the general and oft deserved reputation of being somewhat less than capable students. When my Uncle Ray was a senior at Ole Miss, as I mentioned in another chapter, his academic philosophy had finally evolved into, "Everything above a 'C' is wasted." He could have easily registered straight "A's", had it not been for his fervent opinion.

I adhered to that hypothesis when I got to Ole Miss – out of respect for my mother's brother, of course.

"Yeah, right," I can almost hear you doubt.

The academic environment has changed for the better in these latter years, thanks to a limited number of available football scholarships, NCAA regulations, and the demands of society. Football itself has certainly become more complex, requiring a more intellectual participant. Some football players today may not make good grades, due to a lack of effort, not a shortage of ability.

But the pursuit of academic excellence common today had not yet risen to its present status in the nineteen fifties. Then, as I mentioned in *Walk Carefully Around the Dead*, the accumulation of philosophy regarding grades seemed to be: anyone can study and make good grades; anyone can refuse to study and make bad grades; only a unique student can refuse to study and still make good grades. Unfortunately few did, even with the "enablement" of cheating.

In the mid-Fifties, Ole Miss signed a big and very talented tackle from a small town in South Mississippi to a football scholarship. I'll call him Clyde but that's not his name. As in the former book and this one, names have often been changed in order to protect the guilty.

By the late spring of his freshman year, the talented

tackle, who was much more proficient on the football field than in the classroom, had enrolled in his first philosophy class, introducing him, I suppose, to some measure of abstract thought. Because of that and the fact that he would be flying on an airplane the following fall, Clyde had begun, apparently, to consider actions necessary to survive a plane crash, although he had not voiced his considerations to anyone, at least not to his two traveling companions.

The three teammates were hitchhiking from Oxford to South Mississippi one Friday afternoon, a month or so before the end of the school year. (Few students owned cars in the Fifties, and even fewer football players. Often hitchhiking afforded the only travel to home and back.)

The three wayfarers caught their first ride to Grenada. Clyde, usually very loquacious, was abnormally quiet. In the back seat of their first ride, one of the big athlete's buddies commented, "Clyde, you sure are quiet. Is anything wrong?"

"Naw, I'm just thinkin'."

From Grenada, they caught a ride to Jackson. Clyde remained stoic. His friends wondered about him. One of them asked, "You sure you're alright? You feel bad?"

"Hell, no," the irritated tackle retorted, "I'm thinkin'.."

"Wa'l, you sure are quiet," one of the wondering teammates asserted. "Say something every now and then to let us know you're alive."

At Jackson, the three hitchhiking trekkers climbed into a Hattiesburg-bound car. Clyde said nothing.

They were standing on the side of Highway 49 in Hattiesburg, the two friends with thumbs pointing south. Clyde stood behind them, silent. Suddenly, at the top of his lungs, the awakened giant shouted, "I believe I got it!"

"You believe you've got what?" one of his shocked

companions asked.

"I believe I've got it figured out!"

"What figured out?"

"If a feller' was to jump out of a falling airplane on a board, like a piece of plywood, to 'bout five feet above the ground and then step 'offen it, he wouldn't git hurt!"

The final leg of the journey found the two friends doubled over with laughter and the "sagacious" philosopher wondering why!

"Wal', dammit, he wouldn't!!"

NEVER AGAIN!

When I was preparing to enter counseling, which required 5 years of college and seminary work, I was taught an incredible "truth," which after 25 years of talking to women, I accept without question, nor hard proof. Risking the wrath of many of you, I will articulate the socially incorrect statement, letting the chips fall where they may (no, you can't have my telephone number.)

Men's brains and women's brains differ. I know, I know, that declaration contains the elements of destruction for me, but even so, I believe it. Let me explain what I was taught and what I have come to believe.

Little boys and little girls are born into the world with the two sides of their brains attached by tissue. But little boys are born with the capacity to produce testosterone, which at certain but varying ages they do. The male chemical destroys the connecting tissue, so I have been taught, which means that the two sides of the male brain are thereby disengaged. The woman doesn't experience this phenomenon, thus the two sides of her brain remain connected by that tissue, a bridge easily and instantly crossed.

Since one side of the brain is considered to be the "receiving" side and the other, the "action" side, women discover they can both talk and listen to others talk at the same time. Apparently, most men cannot – I certainly can't! Historically, woman has needed that marvelous gift in order to work in the home and attend to the children simultaneously (times have changed that) and she can alternate concentration from the receiving side to the active side instantaneously.

Man, however, finds switching from one side of his brain to the other to be slower and far more difficult, due to the destroyed connecting tissue. That's one reason, wife, when your husband is driving your family on a trip, he doesn't want to make bathroom stops. He has switched over to the "action" side of his brain. "It's only another hundred miles, Honey, we can all go to the bathroom when we get there."

Without intentionally becoming socially incorrect, therefore, men and women do often think differently. Jackie Simpson's wife certainly discovered that truth – the hard way.

Jackie, an All-American guard from Corinth, married after football season his senior year. He and his wife moved to Vet Village in January, 1958. For those of you who may not remember, Vet Village consisted of barracks type structures, located near the Coliseum where nice brick family residences now stand. They were famous for their paper-thin walls, even between apartments. With little housing in Oxford at the time almost all married students lived there.

One afternoon Jackie's bride asked him to take out the garbage. Apparently Jackie was "on" the action side of his brain, involved in other activity. He didn't respond. She asked him again. He ignored her. A few minutes later he was taking a shower and his new wife yelled the third time,

"Jackie, will you PLEASE take out the garbage?"

With that, Jackie threw the shower door open, walked "drippingly" across the bedroom, and then the kitchen floors, grabbed the garbage can and unceremoniously took it outside to the curb–, without a stitch of clothes on–! Then he reared his head backward, emitted the Tarzan yell while pounding himself on the chest with both fists, and slowly walked back to his apartment, where a shocked, silent, and wide-eyed woman was waiting for him. Even from this chronological distance I can guess that she was thinking – the same thing most wives think at one time or another, "What in the world have I married?"

She never asked him to carry the garbage out again, so the story goes. There may have been a method in his madness.

CHAPTER V

BIG GEORGE

After I retired from pro football, I opened three super-markets: one in Eupora where I lived at the time; one in Fulton; and one in Calhoun City. My secretary answered the telephone in Eupora one day, and I heard her say, "Yes, he is – may I tell him who's calling?"

The year was either 1963 or 1964.

"Paige, a man who calls himself 'Big George' wants to talk to you."

I snatched the phone from her hand, "Big George? The only Big George I have ever heard of is Big George Rhodes!"

"That's me," the gruff voice responded. "What the hell you doin'?"

"Wanting to talk to you."

"I'm on my way over to Eupora right now."

"Where are you?"

"Ackerman. See you in twenty minutes."

I had never met Big George Rhodes, but I had heard of him from football players, from my Uncle Buster Poole, later from dozens of admirers around the Eupora-Ackerman area, and from my father-in-law, for whom George had once worked. He was a Paul Bunyan in blue jeans, a contempo-rary Sampson, without long hair or Delilah.

His booming voice ricocheted off the walls of my store. "Where's Paige?"

Even from my office above the meat market, I heard him. Looking through my one-way window above the floor of my store, I saw Big George moving down the first isle toward the stockroom and the stairs which led to my office. I would have known him even if I had not known he was coming–! He looked exactly like I envisioned – 6 feet tall, 300 pounds, and all muscle, and he more than filled his blue jeans. His shirt sleeves had been removed to accommodate his mammoth arms. He wore cowboy boots and a dirty baseball cap, and his upper body rotated as he walked, in order to move one leg out in front of the other, I suspected. His arms swung at a 45 degree angle from his body, and his forearms looked like two cured hams with 5 fingers each.

George was the strongest man ever to wear the Rebel red and blue – and maybe any other football uniform. He had never lifted an artificial weight.

Five seconds after the giant disappeared from the floor of the store through the stockroom door, I heard his booted foot hit the first stair-step. Without knocking, he threw my office door open, filling the doorway with his gigantic torso.

"Where's that boy who calls his'self Cothren when he's really a Poole?" he bellowed.

"Right here, Big George," I responded, rising from my chair.

By the time I maneuvered from behind my desk, George was standing beside it. I thrust out my anemic right hand, which he ignored. Both of his massive arms suddenly enveloped me, and with little apparent effort, he nudged the ceiling with my head.

"So you're Buster Poole's nephew, huh? Not as big as I thought you'd be," he blurted out, looking up into my face.

"Dynamite comes in –," I whispered with the little air left in my lungs.

"Big packages hold more!" he finished the sentence.

"I agree – I agree!" I wheezed. I never considered contradicting George, having heard enough about him throughout my life to know that.

George lowered me back to the floor. I disciplined the expression of pain from my face and tried not to breathe deeply too quickly. Old football players refuse to admit someone can hurt them.

"You bought the mountain!" he asserted.

"Yep."

"And moved a big log house up on it!"

"Yes, I did."

"I want to see it. I got me a fifth o' corn in my truck. Let's go look at it and have a drink!"

"George, it's in the middle of the day. I don't need to be drinking this early in the ....!"

"Hell, boy, I didn't ask. Since when does Buster Poole's nephew and T. F. Taylor's son-in-law refuse to have a drink with George Rhodes? Come on...!"

I followed him down the stairs and to his pickup.

The mountain, forty acres of land, lay 4 miles northwest of Eupora. Like an inverted ice cream cone, 38 acres rose sharply up 720 feet above sea level to two flat acres on top. It was covered with huge sandstone boulders, some 30 feet or more across. I had bought 2 log cabins, each more than a hundred years old, numbered the logs and reassembled them, on top of the mountain, into one large lodge. It doubled as a weekend retreat for my family and a "party palace" with my friends. From the deck, I could see the lights of Calhoun City, 25 miles to the north; Winona, 30 miles to the west; Starkville, 25 miles to the east; and Eupora to the south, although I gained little joy in gazing upon the lights of one of the towns. (In the late Nineteen Seventies, I gave the 5 bedroom, 3 bath log structure to French Camp Academy, French Camp,

Mississippi. It is now known as French Camp Bed and Breakfast on the Natchez Trace.)

George and I sat in the rustic, cow-skin rocking chairs on my deck. I had drafted two glasses from the kitchen and he poured me a drink – of corn. I hated corn liquor. Wisdom, however, decreed me to drink it.

"I've loved two men in my life, Paige ..."

The words seem to emanate easily from a heart which had seriously, for a while, considered them. They sounded strange to me, coming from that particular source, but that thought, too, I withheld.

"...And you are kin to both of them – Buster Poole and T. F. Taylor. You are the only person in the world kin to both of them — one reason I wanted to meet you."

He smiled. I relaxed – a little.

THE LEGEND

Tom Swayze, college football's and Ole Miss' first full-time athletic recruiter heard about a big, fast fullback playing for Sturgis High School in the little village of Sturgis, Mississippi, located between Ackerman and Starkville. Stories that no one could tackle him cascaded from the little town. It was the late Nineteen Forties, not long after the end of the Second World War.

Because Sturgis lay in Buster's recruiting zone, Tom asked the assistant coach to visit the high school senior. After receiving directions, Buster found the big running back up in the pine-covered hills near the little village, engaged in the profession of his father, logging.

* * * * *

"Damnedest sight I've ever seen, John," Buster reported to Coach Vaught. Rhodes was logging without mules, except to pull the wagon. He picked the smaller pine trees up all at once and put them on the wagon. The bigger ones he loaded one end at a time." (Before mechanized equipment replaced mules, loggers used them to pull logs up ramps onto the log trailer or wagon.)

"Now, Bus," Coach Vaught questioned, "I've never known you to exaggerate. You telling me this boy loaded pine logs by hand?"

"I wouldn't have believed it either, John, if I hadn't seen it, but that was what he was doing."

"How big is he?"

"He's about 5'10" or 5'11". Weighs about 240."

"Is he fat?" – the head coach inquired.

"Not an ounce on him. He's just big."

"Can he move?"

"I talked to his high school coach, and he insists that the boy is fast. Said it takes 3, 4, 5, and sometimes 6 tacklers to bring him down."

"Did you find out much about his personality and family? What about his grades?"

"He's tough. Comes from a logging family. Folks in Sturgis say he'll fight at the drop of a hat, but so far he hasn't gotten crossed with the law. Seems to respect lawmen. But he apparently has one little problem."

"What?"

"He drinks," the assistant answered.

"DRINKS? Hell, how old is he?"

"Eighteen, barely."

"What does he drink?" Vaught inquired.

"Apparently just about anything he can get his hands on –! He's even showed up at football practice and in class a little drunk."

"Well, we can't sign a football player who drinks, Bus. Hell, he'll have every player on the squad drinking. I've never coached a drunk football team."

"I agree, John, but this boy's gonna play college football somewhere – if he wants to – and he's probably gonna be a great one. State's after him, and if we don't sign him, they will. Sturgis is only 15 miles from Starkville."

"Where does Sturgis play Friday night?" Coach Vaught asked.

"At home."

"Watch him Friday night, Buster. Does he want to sign with us?"

"Said he does. I think we're ahead of State."

"Well, we'll decide before signing date. Maybe we can dry him out before he gets here."

BIG GEORGE, A REBEL

"Hell, he's gonna' kill someone Buster, and he doesn't know a damn thing about football."

Bruiser Kinard was debating the assets and liabilities of Big George with Buster. It was the third week of football practice in 1949. The two assistants sat in the coaches' dressing room following a hot and hard workout.

"He's like a Sherman tank," the offensive line coach continued, "attacking bicycles. We don't have three men who can handle him. But I don't believe he'll ever play offense. He's having a little trouble learning the plays. Besides, I think I smelled beer on his breath in practice today."

"I'll talk to him," Buster retorted. "By the way, did you hear what he did in the dorm last night?"

"No, what?"

"The fellows were still laughing about it on the field today. He picked Tank Crawford up under one arm and Showboat Boykin up under the other one and ran up and down the hall with them kicking and screaming. Even ran up and down the stairs – 450 pounds."

"He's by far the strongest man I've ever seen," Bruiser admitted, "even in pro ball. I just wish he were a little smarter, and we could control him. We gotta make him quit drinking."

"You're right," Buster agreed. "Let's move him over to defense. I'll work with him. He'll either become the greatest defensive lineman in the history of this league, and maybe the nation. Or he won't stay here!"

(Note: At the time of George's tenure at Ole Miss, college football employed the use of two platoons. In 1953, it reverted to one platoon. Now, of course, it again uses two platoons.)

IT WAS HOPELESS

Buster worked with Big George the rest of the year and the next one. He coached him; he counseled him; he encouraged him; he drove him; he yelled at him; but he couldn't control him off the field any more than 3 of his teammates could control him on it. Buster couldn't stop him from drinking.

The assistant coach called him into his office.

"George, how do you feel about staying here at Ole Miss?" Bus asked the big lineman.

"I don't know, coach, I don't really like it here."

"You don't like Ole Miss?"

"No, it's not that, coach. I just don't like college. I love Ole Miss, and I 'preciate what you're tryin' to do for me, but I'm out of place here. I tha'nk I'm goin' home. I'm two years behind in my loggin'!"

"I hate to see you do that, George. I would really like to see you stay in school and on the team. You need an education, and you'll play pro football if you want it bad enough. But you have to stop drinking. We can't have any more of that."

"I know, Coach Buster, but I can't stop. And I want to git to loggin' again. That's what I want to do."

"I wish you would think about it, George."

"Naw, coach, I'm goin' home."

Big George Rhodes went home.

George had been back in Sturgis only a few days when he met an Ole Miss graduate, an attorney friend on the street.

"George," the friend exclaimed, "what are you doing home? You're supposed to be at Ole Miss practicing ball!"

"I quit!"

"You quit? You quit school?"

"Yeah."

"What happened?" the lawyer inquired.

"I had trouble with my books!"

"Your books? Which one?"

"That big RED 'un."

For the next 20 years George logged, drank whiskey, and "cleaned out" night clubs, from the Tennessee line to Jackson, from the Alabama line to the Mississippi River. He became a legend known by all the law enforcement officers and feared by almost all good ole beer-drinking boys.

Occasionally strangers moved into the area and challenged Big George, remonstrances which always ended exactly as all the local people knew they would.

Chubby Ellis, former Lowndes County Supervisor who played football with George at Ole Miss remembers him well, both on the field and later.

"George used to come to Columbus and get drunk, when I was county supervisor. The police would arrest him and then call me to come get him out of jail, which I always did."

For all of his strength and drinking, Big George was surprisingly hard to anger. And he never fought police, culling, however, no one else.

"One night at a joint, Big George picked up the owner by the legs," Chubby continued, "and squeezed him so hard he broke the man's thigh bone – accidentally. He was just playing around."

Later, during the time George helped clear the Pearl River Bottom for the construction of the Ross Barnett Reservoir, the police arrested an extremely aggressive drunk, whom they had difficulty controlling even after they put him in a jail cell. Knowing Big George and conscious of the fact that he was working in the area, the law enforcement officers found him in a local beer joint and arrested him for a reason known only to them. George, who was accustomed to being arrested, went without resistance. The hopeful police deposited the huge logger in the cell with the fierce prisoner, knowing sooner or later the drunk's anger would force him to challenge George. It happened sooner than later and before long the indignant culprit was screaming for police protection. After eliciting from him an assurance that passivity had now replaced his antagonism, the officers withdrew Big George from the cell, escorted him back to the sanctity of the beer joint, and thanked him.

"Anytime," the strong one replied.

TO HAVE A DRINK

The sun was setting as Big George and I finished his bottle of corn whiskey. He wiped his mouth with the back of his powerful hand and bellowed, "Got anything else to drank out here, Paige?"

"Got some beer in the refrigerator, some Canadian Club and some Old Charter. Which one you want?"

"Old Charter first, then we'll kill the other."

"Gonna' take a big killing, George. There are four or five fifths in there."

"No problem!" he promised.

And there was none.

A couple of fifths later, Big George, his coarse voice softened by the alcohol or sentimentality, slowly turned his unshaven face toward me. It was dark. Bull bats dove against the shadowy sky, seeking insects which migrated toward the lights of the cabin. Whippoorwills had begun their nightly serenade, aiming their haunting calls at us — *Chip fell out of the white oak – Chip fell out of the white oak.*" The leaves of the trees which surrounded the cabin grew silent, subdued by the still humid air of a Mississippi summer night, and the smell of honeysuckle drifted slowly through the stillness.

Light from inside the cabin glanced off the side of George's somber face. A large tear welled up in the huge man's eye and slowly slid down his cheek, golden and visible because of the light.

"I love Buster Poole," the giant uttered softly. "He tried to help me. If I had stayed at Ole Miss, Buster would have made an All-American out of me, and I coulda' played pro ball. I shoulda' listened to him."

"He still talks about you, George. He says you are the strongest man he has ever seen – by far."

For a full minute neither of us said anything. Finally George spoke. "Guess I'd better go now, Paige."

Somehow Big George maneuvered his truck back down the mountain, dodging the pine trees and large boulders which lined the narrow road. A few minutes later he pulled up behind my Corvette which was still parked at the store. I was opening the door when George grabbed my left arm, his Herculean fingers digging into my bicep, which I flexed to reduce the pain, futilely.

"You listen to him, Paige!"

"Beg your pardon?"

"Buster – you listen to him."

"I'll listen to him, Big George; I'll listen to him."

I watched the tail lights of George's pickup truck move south on Highway 9, cross Highway 82, and disappear around a curve. I never saw him again.

Once or twice a year for the following several years, though, the former Rebel would call me. He always ended the conversation, whether sober or drunk, with an emphatic command and proclamation.

"You listen to yo' Uncle Buster, you hear, Paige? I wish I had!"

A few years after I met him, Big George Rhodes died – the strongest man ever to wear the Red and Blue. Still ringing in my ears at age 63 are his words, which many times I too wished I had heeded.

"You listen to him, now you hear!"

I still don't know if I promised Big George I would listen to Buster because I believed in the trustworthiness of my Uncle's wise and protective counsel or because I found disagreeing with him to be very – well – uncomfortable. One thing I do know, Big George was right.

CHAPTER VI

THE MEATHEAD

When pressed on the subject, those of us who played football at Ole Miss in the late Forties, Fifties, and early Sixties admit quickly that the game has changed. Indeed players grow bigger and run faster today generally than in our day, although not without exceptions. Earl Blair with whom I played in the 1950's ran less than a ten flat hundred, as did Billy Yelverton, a six foot, four inch, 220 pound lineman. Today, size opens the holes and speed gains the yardage. Earlier, toughness and maneuverability accomplished the two feats.

Toughness, which included playing with cuts, bruises, and occasionally broken bones, in the day of limited substitution, catapulted players through brutal three-hour workouts twice a day, playing both offense and defense in 100 degree heat – without water. Following the practices, toughness enabled us to run ten 50-yard sprints, ten 100-yard sprints, and suffer through fifteen minutes of accursed grass drills led by Assistant Coach Bruiser Kinard – down-up-down-back-up-down-back-front-up, etc.

I would love to witness a 240 pound lineman carrying 320 pounds try to do that!!

Toughness opened the holes, and maneuverability gained the yardage. Players needed to be "shifty" as the sports writers then identified the characteristic. Speed was good but shiftiness was demanded – of all half-backs and pass receivers. Interestingly the fullback, considered to be more of a lineman than a back, escaped the requirement to be shifty, but he had to be tough. When he ran the ball, he tried to run over people not around them.

Even as we old-timers must admit that football players

today move faster and mount larger, we must also confess that sophistication and complexity have replaced simplicity in offensive and defensive systems. The coaches never even issued playbooks to the players in the earlier days at Ole Miss, teaching everything on the field in the timeless workouts. Today, limited practicing rules combined with ever-evolving complicated challenges force coaches to employ computers in establishing offenses and defenses.

Currently defensive teams sometimes initiate the defense AFTER the offense snaps the ball, requiring all the defensive players to recognize the offensive tactic immediately and in unison. The same may be demanded of the offensive team, as 11 players diagnose changes in defensive alignments, including line-backer bliltzes, linemen stunts, and altered coverages of defensive backs, after snapping the ball.

Other latter-day deviations in the sport occur OFF the field, though, like conflicts with the law – and grades.

Until a few years ago, I had never personally known nor even heard of a football player in trouble with the law, I don't think! (As soon as I wrote that, I thought, "Surely there was someone–!") The two, playing football and breaking the law, were antimony – opposites which in my youth simply did not co-exist. Of course, today that has changed, as proven by O. J. Simpson and many others.

When my mother, who was surrounded by 14 college football relatives, including three brothers and a son, finally commented on the O. J. tragedy, she said in her normal, soft, loving voice, "I know it does look pretty bad for him, but I don't believe he did it. You know, he WAS a football player."

That's right, Mother!!

Just joking! I believe he did it, and so does she now.

If, when I played football at Ole Miss, I had stolen

something or committed a felony, my greatest fear would have emanated from Buster Poole and the other coaches, not the law. But then, passing decades have eroded the coaches' control of the players and undermined their authority, so that little fear of them now resides in many players.

THE GRADES

Today, with limited scholarships, football players MUST pass their courses. We had to pass too, but with 50 to 100 freshmen football scholarships given each year, the issue was less critical. I suppose, given our attitudes toward studying, colleges were fortunate to be able to sign so many athletes. Losing a player to academic failure didn't cripple a team then like it does today.

And we lost some to academic failure. That's why the athletic department assigned tutors to many of us, which I will discuss later.

Concerning football players and studying, I mentioned in *Walk Carefully Around the Dead* that an enigmatic attitude evolved, perhaps flowing through those returning to Ole Miss from the battlefields of World War II, and passed on to ensuing classes. Anyone can study and pass and anyone can refuse to study and fail, but it takes a special person to pass WITHOUT studying. I mentioned that might necessitate cheating. Those athletes who adopted that philosophy came to be known as meatheads.

Many of those boys who left the playing field of Ole Miss for the bloody battlefields of Europe and the Pacific, came back to Oxford as men. Studying for knowledge and good grades, I imagine, seemed frivolous to them, following four years of facing death.

Chubby Ellis, a player in the late Forties, elaborates.

"In the Spring of 1948, Charlie (Roach) Conerly (who fought in the Pacific) and Tom (Tip Toe) Hardy had a course in the Graduate Building. They were both struggling to pass the course but not wanting to study, they were having difficulty. They put their heads together and came up with an idea."

Seems that the two found the janitor who cleaned the building and advised him that the professor's mimeograph copies thrown into the waste basket were worth money. The two veteran athletes struck a deal with him. Each night, they visited the janitor at home and bought their guaranty.

Roach and Tip Toe were passing comfortably when final exam time rolled around, and they went to get their copy. This time, though, the janitor told them that he hadn't gotten it.

"They damn near fainted," Chubby continued. "They had picked the janitor up in Tom's old car, and they were riding around. After refusing to let him out of the car and threatening him, they suspected he was stalling for more money, so they raised the ante."

As soon as they did that, the old man pulled a crumpled piece of paper from his trousers and exclaimed, "Wal' look here! I believe this IS what you boys are looking for."

The future All-Pro quarterback and his college teammate made A's in the course.

In their own words, "Hotty-Toddy!"

"In 1948," Chubby remembers, "I was going with a good-looking girl from South Florida, who had come to Ole Miss. She had spent so much time partying that she was about to flunk out of school, and it was already exam week."

Chubby and a few other football players, southern gentlemen all, began to search for some way to get the exams for her.

One night the search squad was slipping behind the old cafeteria toward a classroom building when the campus police spotted them. They started running. "Ben (Puny) Mann was running faster than all of us, hollering 'don't run – don't run!' " Chubby laughed. "Hell, he was leading the pack and hollering 'don't run!'

"Finally we got to the hedge which surrounded the building and like high divers in the summer Olympics, we plunged headfirst under it. Red Jenkins dived into a broken bottle and cut his hand so badly we took him to the hospital to have it sewed up – after the police left, of course."

Chubby and his companions spent all of that night trying to steal exams for the co-ed and at the hospital so they never studied for their own exams. "Course, we probably wouldn't have anyway," confessed the athlete.

The next day, the three of them were "taking" Dr. Morse's Geology exam, sitting side by side on the back row of the classroom, their minds blank. "We didn't know a damn thing," Chubby admitted. "A young fellow, a good student, sitting directly in front of us, whispered that he had finished the exam. 'No, you haven't,' declared Puny, as he thrust his exam up to him. 'Fill this one out!' After he finished Puny's exam, Red and I gave him ours, and he filled them out. The kid took four exams that day and made A's on all of them."

That same year some of the World War II veteran athletes took an accounting course in the Lyceum. Carpenters were working on the building and timbers were protruding from the third floor windows. It was exam time. The football players decided to steal the exam.

"Of course the prof's third floor office door was locked," one of the group remembered, "so we climbed out of a hall window and carefully walked on the timbers all the way around to his office window, which we found open."

The spies couldn't find the exam, but they did discover the Prof's grade book, so they took it back to the athletic dorm and commissioned an artist from the athletic ranks, who practiced imitating the professor's numbers and letters. After retrieving ink eradicator, they gave themselves good grades, but they didn't stop there.

"Who do we want to fail?" one of them asked the group.

"That little pip-squeak up in the front row who's always shooting off his mouth," someone else replied. "Let's flunk him."

"Man, get smart. We can't flunk him," another countered. "The Prof will know SOMETHING'S wrong."

Late that night, the reconnoiters replaced the grade book back into the prof's office. "But we made such low grades on the exam," one of them admitted, "we had to go back the next night and change our exam grades."

"How were your final grades?" I asked the old confiscator.

"Hell, we ALL made good grades in THAT class!"

* * * * *

My Uncle Ray Poole also served his country in the South Pacific. After the war, he too returned to Ole Miss, in the Fall of '46, to play his last year of college football. I was a boy of eleven and, like a branding iron pressed against the flank of a young steer, his philosophy of studying and grades burned a permanent effigy into my young impressive mind.

At the end of the school year, Ray came home having registered "C's" in all his courses – for an entire year, both semesters. When asked by a relative how he managed to make nothing but C's, he quickly and with ample seriousness responded, "EVERYTHING ABOVE A 'C' IS WASTED!"

I tried in vain to implement that principle while in high school. Mother rejected it. I was forced to wait until college.

I made good grades in high school, finishing third in Natchez High's 1952 graduating class. I didn't want to disappoint my Mother, who believed against truth, that I was smart.

But then I enrolled in college.

I left my Mother in Natchez.

I encountered the professors of Ole Miss.

Football players in my days at the University categorized our teachers into two divisions – football friendly and football unfriendly. By the time I entered the registration line my Freshman year, I had tucked away comfortably in the front pocket of my blue jeans a list of the football friendly ones. But I failed to get one for my first-year economics class.

"How many football players do we have in here?" the economics prof asked the first day of class.

"Boy, this is great," I murmured to a team-mate. "My football-friendly professor didn't even ask that!"

Five or six of us raised our hands.

"Now, I want you to stand up and move to the back of the room and let students have your seats."

I grew up some that day. My high school teachers had almost begged me to study and seemed hurt if I didn't.

I also got mad that day and I stood up abruptly, grabbed my books from the desk, and briskly wove my way through the "students" to the back of the room. "I'll show you, you son-of-a-b—h," I thought, "I just won't study for your class."

And I didn't! Nor for anyone else's. I became a meathead, pure, undiluted, committed – for four years. I EARNED the name.

Years later, after I got my master's degree and was teaching in Bible College, I ran into a former team-mate at a Rebel football game.

"Paige," he exclaimed, "I haven't seen you lately. What are you doing now?"

"Well, – I'm teaching."

Surprise enveloped his wide-eyed face.

"TEACHING? – WHERE?"

"At a college in Memphis."

"College? You're teaching in college?" He looked at his wife expectantly. Her face, too, was blank.

"Yes."

"What are you teaching?"

"You mean what courses?"

"Yeah, what courses, what classes do you teach?!"

"Well, I teach the Gospel of John, Personal Evangelism and Doctrine, in the daytime. I teach another course at night to about a hundred people."

He choked. A second or two later with hoarse voice he asked, "What course at night?"

I didn't want to tell him. He looked healthy, but I really couldn't know–!

Meekly I answered, "Greek."

"GREEK? THE LANGUAGE?"

"Yes."

My friend hesitated for a moment or two, grasped his wife's arm and turned quickly. As they walked away, he glanced toward her and tried unavailingly to talk softly, "Boy, if I didn't believe in God before, I sure believe in Him NOW!"

MR. CERNY

When I signed up for the accounting class, I had absolutely no idea what the class involved, though not because my knowledge enveloped the principle of the course, but fell short of the intricacies thereof. I knew nothing about the principle either.

I asked my team-mate and room-mate Jerry McKaskel, "What is accounting?"

"Paige, you don't even know what it is?"

"No," I responded sarcastically. "I didn't grow up in the city like you – I grew up in the country."

"What's that got to do with it?"

"You know what ACCOUNTING is, ROOMIE – you figure THAT out."

I don't think Jerry ever bothered to explain it to me, but Mr. Joe Cerny, my accounting prof tried to –! "How many of you took bookkeeping in high school?" he asked.

I couldn't raise my hand. Almost everyone else did.

"Paige, you've never had any bookkeeping?"

"No, sir!"

"Stand up and move to this desk right here." Mr. Cerny pointed to a vacant desk immediately in front of his. "Scoot your desk up until it touches mine."

I obeyed.

"Now, that's where I want you when you come in here, your desk touching mine. I want to see your eyeballs for 50 minutes, three times a week."

"How can I take a nap sitting up here, Mr. Cerny?"

He bellowed, "You're NOT going to take a nap in HERE. You're going to learn accounting."

Mr. Cerny was a huge man, at least six feet four inches tall and about 250 pounds, with a full head of black hair, in spite of his age, and a sparkle in his eye. He spoke with a booming voice even within the closed confines of the classroom, and not knowing better, one might be a little afraid of him. But I knew him, and I liked him – even more important to me, I knew he liked me.

A week later I sat in Coach Junie Hovious' office, the member of Vaught's staff who arranged academic help for football players.

"Coach, I need tutors."

"For which classes?"

"Well, for all of them, but especially for my accounting class."

"Who's your teacher?"

"Mr. Cerny."

"He'll be fair with you. What's the problem?"

"I gotta do something called practice sets. I don't think I can! I need help."

"I'll see what I can do."

* * * * *

"Come in!" I had just walked into my room after supper, following a long, hard workout, the first week of September, 1955. We were playing Georgia the 17th in Atlanta, and we had less than two and a half weeks to prepare. On the coaching staff, mission had replaced mercy, if any had existed, and anxiety had nudged aside compassion. I was tired and lying on my bed.

The knock on my dorm door sounded a little tentative,

as though the intruder thought he might not be fully welcome. He was right.

"Come in," I reluctantly invited, aware that I had deliberately lowered the sound of "in" an octave from "come."

"Paige, I'm your tutor. Coach Hovious sent me to help you with accounting."

The tutor looked a little older than I. A slight smile, more reserved than confident, adorned his pleasant face, a twinkle enlightened his eyes. He stood about 6 feet tall, 150 pounds. His slacks and button-up shirt were more conservative than those of 1950's football players, and I wondered if he was thinking, "Yep, another meathead I'm going to hafta make look smart."

As quickly as my exhausted mind produced that disconcerting thought, however, it issued another one – "I don't give a damn what he or anyone else thinks. I gotta pass accounting."

"Are you a student?" I asked. A wider grin swept across his friendly face.

"Grad student."

"Oh? – in what?"

"Accounting."

"Wow," I thought. "Is Coach Hovious a great guy or what? My troubles are over!" and I was right until – well – until the final exam, at the end of the semester.

Mr. Cerny gave no quizzes nor tests except the final exam. We turned in homework and the finished practice sets for 65 percent of our grade. The final exam was worth 35 percent. Going into the final, my tutor and I sported a very high "A".

I thumbed through the exam, about 20 pages of questions relating to accounting problems and principles. I recognized nothing.

"You have two hours," Mr. Cerny reminded us. "When you finish, write your name on the exam and leave it on my desk."

He was looking directly at me!

I thumbed through the exam again, slower this time. I still recognized nothing.

Every other student seemed to be working feverishly. My lifeless exam lay quietly closed upon my desk, my lethargic hands resting beside it. I lifted my doleful gaze from the mystical pages into the emphatic face of my professor, only five feet away. He was staring directly at me, amused. "Mr. Cerny, I don't know the answer to a single question, and I can't work any of the problems," I defiantly blurted out, loud enough for everyone in the class to hear. Controlled snickers followed my bellicose declaration, and I turned my head slightly. They stopped. Then I re-attached my stare onto my professor's face, and waited expectantly for his ruling.

For a full 30 seconds, Mr. Cerny looked at me intently. I thought I saw a slight smile elevate the corners of his mouth, but I could have been wrong.

"You throw in the towel for a "C", Paige?"

Like the urgent hands of a mother pulling a child from an on-coming car, I seized my exam and like a Florida hurricane ripping the tin roof from a Key Largo bungalow, I flung the blank papers onto my patient professor's desk. They slid all the way across it, hit him in the chest, and fell into his lap.

He laughed!

I rejoiced!

Then my forbearing teacher placed the exam on his

desk, reached for his red pen, planted a large "C" on the first page and, instituted it the initial paper of the forthcoming stack.

I smiled gratefully, stood up, and prepared to leave. "Where do you think you're going, Paige?"

"I'm through, Mr. Cerny," I retorted, "I'm leaving."

"No, you aren't!"

"I can't leave?"

"Not now," he threatened. "You can leave later."

"When?"

"When the last person has turned his paper in."

"Mr. Cerny, that'll be almost two hours!"

"Sit down, Paige, and be quiet."

"Awe, Mr. Cerny!"

Five boring minutes later, I whispered, "Mr. Cerny?"

The provoked professor looked up at me. He said nothing, and the corners of his mouth had settled back down into their non-amused position.

I kept my voice low. "Can I go over to the Grill and get a newspaper?" I heard snickers again.

Mr. Cerny hesitated for a few seconds. "You can go, Paige, but you have to come back here within ten minutes. If you don't, that "C" is going to deflate to an "F".

"I'll be back," I murmured.

And I was –! At the end of the two hours, I still knew no accounting, but I had almost memorized that day's *Commercial Appeal* sports page and comics.

* * * * *

By the late 1960's, I had finished my professional football career and owned three Piggly Wiggly supermarkets, along with several other businesses. Because I lived in Eupora, I built my home office into the grocery store located there. The massive amount of accounting involved, before computers, forced me to hire a secretary who could also keep books. I constructed her office and mine above the meat market.

I had not seen Mr. Cerny in ten years.

"Paige – how are you?"

Standing at the front of the Eupora store near a checkout counter, I heard his unmistakable booming voice. Turning quickly, I looked directly into the face of my former accounting professor, who quickly strode toward me, thrusting out a huge hand, a warm smile upon his aging face.

"Fine, Mr. Cerny," I responded, "How are YOU doing, and what in the world are you doing in Eupora, Mississippi?"

Turning my hand loose, he continued walking toward the rear of the store. I quickly followed.

"I'm fine, too, and I came to look at your books. Where's your office?"

"You're going in the right direction, Mr. Cerny. We have to go through the stock room. It's above the meat market."

"Most of them are," he knowingly concluded.

I raced to keep up with him, and he took the stairs two steps at a time. Opening my office door ahead of me, he plunged in–!

"Sandra, this is Mr. Cerny, my accounting teacher at Ole Miss. Mr. Cerny, this is Sandra."

"How do you do, young lady? Would you get me the books, please?"

110

Sandra looked at me. "Would you please get them, Sandra?"

My secretary questioningly handed them to my professor.

"Now," Mr. Cerny urged, "Would the two of you please go somewhere else for a while? I'm going to need the whole office."

"Ah, – yes sir. When would you like for us to come back?"

"I'll come down when I'm through," he concluded, as he dropped my books onto the carpeted floor and sprawled out beside them.

"Yes, sir. Would you like something to drink – or to eat?"

"No! Thank you."

Sandra and I were sacking groceries when the traveling accountant reappeared.

"Walk out to my car with me, Paige," the professor beseeched.

"Pretty good books, Paige." We were almost to his car. "That young lady is a fine bookkeeper. Tell her that for me."

"THAT YOUNG LADY!! Why do you think SHE keeps the books, Mr. Cerny? I COULD be keeping them!!" He was looking intently into my face, and it was 1955 – I was sitting 5 feet away from him. The corners of his mouth arched upward and a smile spread across his grandfatherly face, a smile which suddenly surrendered to a deep body-rending laugh – "Ho - Ho - Ho - Ho – !"

Mr. Cerny was still laughing, his window rolled down, waving as he pulled out of my parking lot onto Highway 9 and turned his car North toward Oxford.

I yelled as he turned into traffic, "Good to see you again, Mr. Cerny."

I never saw him again.

A GOOD LOOK AT A PROFESSOR'S FEET

I would never have taken a math or math related course had it not been required for a BBA, Bachelor of Business Administration, degree. And I would never have gotten a BBA degree had it not been for my uncle Bus.

Actually my concerned uncle insisted, my freshman year, that I enroll in Pre-Pharmacy. But when those professors recognized the fact that I had never taken high school Chemistry, they placed me in a three-hour lab designed to at least familiarize me with pharmacy terminology. The lab met on Tuesday afternoons from 3:00 to 6:00. So did football practice. I needed no college degree to know I couldn't be in two places at the same time, so I withdrew from the only one I could. I dreaded facing my uncle.

"Uncle Bus, I need to talk to you." He was dressing for practice.

"Can it wait until after practice? We have to be on the field in fifteen minutes."

"Yes, sir, it can, I guess, but I would really like to – uh – uh!"

"Get it over with?"

"Yes, sir."

"What is it?"

"I quit pharmacy school."

"YOU WHAT?"

"I quit pharmacy school."

"WHY?"

"Well, I had to take a catch-up lab, and it meets on Tuesdays from 3:00 to 6:00 and –."

"Paige, you have to enroll in school. You can't even practice much less play in games 'til you do. Since apparently you aren't going to be a pharmacist, do you have any idea what you'd like to study?"

"No, sir. I guess I'll be a coach and teacher."

"No," my uncle countered, "you don't need to be a coach. What about business school?"

"I don't know."

"You need to be in business school. Practice today, but be enrolled before practice tomorrow. See Dean Dunham. He's head of the business school."

"Yes, sir."

* * * * *

"Go!"

I was already crawling.

The math class was so large, it met in the Chemistry building auditorium, which sloped down from the entrance behind the seats to the podium area in front of them. A 10-foot aisle area had been left between the back seats and the wall, in which the doors into and out of the room were located.

Within the first ten minutes of my first class, I had already surveyed the room and discovered that a crawler would be hidden from the professor who stood some 8 feet lower, at the podium, by the backs of the back seats and the students who sat in them. To crawl out of the class after the roll was taken, I would need to accomplish two feats: first, sit on the back row; second, enlist the help of other students who would say "go" when the teacher faced the blackboard, with his back toward the class, and "stop" when he turned back around.

The semester was half over, and I had crawled out of every class – about fifteen other students helped me.

I was on my way again.

"Stop." I stopped.

A few seconds later I heard "go", and I got to the door.

"Stop."

"Go." I quickly pushed the swinging door open and crawled to freedom outside, quietly easing the door shut behind. Still on my knees, I quickly turned my head away from the closed door and looked directly down on a pair of brown shoes, no more than 12 inches from my head. My eyes followed the legs up past the knees, past the waist, past the tie, and into the stern, stoic face of Dean Clive Dunham.

"Howdy do, Dean Dunham. How you?" as I rose quickly to my nervous feet.

"Fine, Paige, how are you?"

"Fine."

I was out of the building within 5 seconds. I was out of the course immediately.

THEY WOULDN'T BELIEVE ME

By the time I enrolled as a freshman at Ole Miss in the Fall of 1953, the term "meathead," which had been assigned to football players by the non-athletic students, had become a badge of honor. Most of the players wore the word proudly, as though it presented the notion, "I passed my courses at Ole Miss without even studying. YOU had to study to pass, Frat

Cat, so in the final analysis, I may actually be smarter than YOU. And I had to do it playing football."

Of course, had graduation been the end, and not the means to an end, the effect, not the cause, that thesis might have been correct. But of course, success in the world requires knowledge, work, and timing. For many of us, much knowledge was lost – forever.

I failed to graduate with my class in the Spring of 1957. I was short one math class and a whole bunch of awesome critters called quality points. So after my first season with the Rams, I went back to Ole Miss, helped coach in Spring practice and registered for 15 hours of classes – 5 courses, 3 hours each – 3 graduate courses and repeats of the discussed math class and Economic Statistics.

Before the classes began, I visited each instructor. The first visit went something like this.

"Professor, I've enrolled in your class."

"Um-huh."

"For four years here I didn't study."

"Um-huh."

"But I want you to know THIS semester, I'm going to study. I'm going to prove to you I'm no longer pure meathead."

"Humh!"

And I did study. I finished with three "A's" and 2 "B pluses", pearls cast before swine, a bottle of Chardonnay at a hot dog stand. I think my unexpected venture into intellectualism drew more looks of suspicion than my well-established rejection of it, and I left my beloved school, graduated, one class behind, and satisfied.

CHAPTER VII

ON THE FIELD

After I completed *Walk Carefully Around the Dead*, I thought, often out loud, "There cannot exist many other on-the-field funny stories about Ole Miss football players and coaches during the 40's, 50's, and 60's. Of course as I mentioned in the Preface and Introduction to this book, numerous other players wrote, called, and stopped me on the street to offer new and equally humorous tales. I included about half of them in this chapter.

Some of the following accounts may, upon first reading, sound slightly familiar. That emanates from two facts: first, the era was practically the same and second, the coaches were exactly the same.

IT'LL DO IT TO YOU

Perhaps nowhere does the 1990's brand of Ole Miss football differ more from the 1950's version than in the area of matrimony, marriage. Current football players may marry – we couldn't, by decree of the coaches.

Reasons existed, we were told, for the rule. Worrying about the welfare of a family might hinder a player's performance on the playing field.

That makes sense – I think.

Marriage contains sex. Sex drains the strength from football players, hindering their performance on the playing field.

For a while THAT made no sense!

Pepper Thomas changed that.

"Uh oh," I can hear some of you say. "Ol' Paige is

about to wade into the deep water of literary verbosity, and drown. Probably another one of those stories which shouldn't be told."

That would be true except for a rare intelligent act on my part. I received Pepper's permission to tell the story. I'm fairly confident he won't kill me. I'm not certain about his wife of forty-five years. Juanita may kill us both.

Pepper Thomas, from Newton, Mississippi, current director of the Ole Miss Golf Course, was one of the top football recruits in the Spring of 1953, a tough little halfback, who was very fast and surprisingly strong for his size. He was also one of three ball carriers to run over me on a football field, the other two being fullback Charlie Flowers in practice at Ole Miss one day and Chicago Cardinal, Ollie Matson, who returned one of my L.A. Rams kick-offs for a touchdown. Pepper smeared me in the Mississippi High School All-Star game on a sweep around the South's left defensive end. I was supposed to contain him and then tackle him. I did neither.

Like other football players who earned football scholarships at Ole Miss in 1953, Pepper wasn't supposed to get married – but he did, and he tried to keep it a secret from the coaches, which he succeeded in doing for a few days. He couldn't, however, hide the fact from his teammates. By the time the day of this story rolled around, we were already kidding him about his changed physical appearance.

"Look a little peaked, Pepper."

"Man, you've drained all the color out of your face."

"You're all shriveled up, Pepper! How much weight you lost?"

"That all you do when you're with her?"

"Damn, Pepper, give her a rest!"

Had it happened late in the practice when everyone

was tired, maybe the coaches wouldn't have discovered his secret for a while longer, but it occurred in the first twenty minutes on a relatively cool day. We were practicing punt returns.

"Pepper, you and McKaskel get back there and return the next one. Come on, let's go, get the lead out," Coach John Cain barked.

The two punt returners assumed their positions some forty yards down field from the line of scrimmage. "Return right" had been called.

Eagle Day arched the punt high, far down the field and the ball turned over just as one well-kicked is supposed to do. McKaskel, the right-returner, caught the ball cleanly and sprinted to his left toward Pepper, who was running toward him. The new husband received the handoff smoothly from his counterpart and raced with great speed for the right side-line, some twenty-five yards away, where a wall of blockers was beginning to form. By the time, however, he turned upfield between the sideline and his protectors, who by now had given him a clean line to the goal-line, the huffing half-back had slowed considerably.

One of his "compassionate" teammates later remarked, "Looked like someone threw a 50-pound sack of 'sex' on his back." (Actually a word other than 'sex' was used.)

Twenty yards downfield the fatigued runner's sprint depreciated to a walk.

"What the hell's wrong with you, Pepper?" a coach yelled. "Run!"

Thirty yards downfield, the weary ball-carrier sank to his knees – but he didn't quit. With football under arm, and lungs laboring for air, the football player crawled on his knees for another five yards, at which point he flopped to the ground on his face, midst the ovation and cheers of his compatriots.

"P——whipped, P——whipped, Pepper is P—— whipped."

"What the hell they talkin' about?" a coach inquired.

A few days later the exhausted one told them.

BUT THEY WERE MARINES

When Jack Cavin, an old buddy of mine from Crosby, got to Ole Miss, it was for him, like many of us, a dream come true. Jack was a very muscular six feet two inch, 215 pound end, big for his day, especially for a freshman. Four years of eating at the athletic training table would put even more weight on him, the rigorous workouts designed to maneuver the additional weight into muscle.

Jack's size was a great attribute but it wasn't his only one. He was fast and he was gung ho, determined to become a starter, first on Wobble's freshman team, then on Coach Vaught's varsity. And like almost all the rest of us, he was nervous – he was a freshman at Ole Miss.

"Being at Ole Miss and a freshman, I was really looking forward to our first practice, but I was scared," the big end remembered.

Fear often produces compulsive behavior. Barney Fife on the Andy Griffith show, when afraid and asked a question would quickly exclaim in his high-pitched, nervous voice, "Yep," regardless of whether or not "Yep" was the right answer.

"Wobble, that first morning, told all the ends to line up on a certain spot on the field," Jack continued. "Nine ends gathered together. Then he said, 'All right ends line up here, and left ends over here.' Eight of the nine were right ends. I was going to be real smart, so I lined up on the left side even though I was a right end."

Two or three of the right ends wanted to move over to the left, obviously realizing that Jack, being the only left end, would offer less competition for a starting position.

"No," Wobble commanded, "get back over there, we only have one left end."

Jack faced the practice alone. It was the first day of September, 1955, and the temperature by practice time, 9:00 AM, had already reached ninety degrees plus. The few puffy white clouds which hung overhead were anchored to a baby blue sky, stilled by air which refused to move.

"It was hot," Jack recalled vividly, for obvious reasons, "and humid. I ran all pass patterns that morning, all running plays, and then after the main workout ended, twenty 20-yard sprints, ten 50-yard sprints, and seven 100-yard sprints. And then we did grass drills. I died."

When the grass drills ended, Jack couldn't walk so he rolled off the field to a mud puddle left by the sprinkler system where he was lying when Wobble walked by.

"Get up and get off the field, Jack."

"I can't, Coach, I can't move," the exhausted end wheezed.

"What do you mean you can't move?"

"Coach, I want to, but I just can't move. I can't make my legs work."

"Can't make your legs work? You don't need to make your legs work to get off the field. I saw two marines in the South Pacific crawl a half-mile with no legs. Surely to God you can get your ass off this field!"

"I crawled to the dressing room," Jack recalled, "and then to bed."

At practice that afternoon, Wobble moved two right ends over to the left end position. Jack was elated.

"I love Wobble," Jack exclaimed. "He saved my life."

WHAT DO YOU THINK I'M RUNNING HERE?

When I'm introduced to young people and they discover the years I played football, often they look sympathetically into my aging face and declare, "Oh, you played in leather helmets!"

"Well, yes," I reluctantly admit, "in high school. But at Ole Miss, we played in plastic."

Plastic helmets were as popular with the players in the fifties as the tear-a-way jerseys I wrote about in *Walk Carefully Around the Dead* had been with our coaches. They were, of course, inferior to the headgear worn by today's players, which are packed with sponge rubber. Our helmets featured two wide canvas straps on the inside, crossing at the center. The straps were hard and unforgiving, but they kept our heads from crashing into the plastic, that is until they broke, which they sometimes did.

The Ole Miss Freshmen were playing at Vanderbilt in the fall of 1954. Wobble Davidson was the coach. Jackie Simpson, from Corinth, later to win All-American honors and both play and coach in the NFL, played guard.

Vanderbilt's best running back was Phil King, who later played with the New York Giants. In the third quarter Phil and Jackie crashed head on, and the canvas strap in Jackie's helmet broke. His head slammed against the top of the headpiece and the front of the helmet scraped all the meat off the top of his nose.

"Everyone got off the pile," teammate Don Barkley remembered, "and Jackie was on the very bottom. When his strap broke, the lick almost knocked him out. We helped him to his feet and revived him, but his head was all the way up in his helmet – you couldn't even see his eyes. Blood was flowing down his face. When he lifted the front of the helmet up, the skin was gone from his nose and the cartilage was showing."

Jackie knew better than to leave the field though. In those days of limited substitutions, once he left the field, he couldn't return in that quarter. Besides, a player only left a game then by the invitation of the coach. So he pushed his helmet back, got into his lineman's stance and took another lick on his strapless helmet which promptly slammed against the top of his head and his already skinned nose.

"Three or four plays later," Don recalled, "Jackie decided any retribution Wobble inflicted on the sideline would be better than what he was suffering on the field. Pushing his helmet up so he could see, he jogged cautiously toward the Ole Miss bench. Wobble met him ten yards out on the field."

"Where the hell do you think you're going, Simpson?"

"Coach, I broke my helmet. I need another one."

"Get your ass back on that field! What do you think I'm running over here – a haberdashery?"

"Jackie had to wait until a time out was called before he could get a new headgear," Don concluded. "He played at least fifteen plays blind, his head so far up in his helmet he couldn't even see. And when you looked at his nose, all you could see was cartilage and blood. The skin and meat were gone."

HOW DID YOU DO THAT?

For twenty years, following the 1953 football season, freshmen football players weren't allowed to play for the varsity. But in 1953 they could and I did, the only freshman at Ole Miss that year to do so. I kicked off for the varsity but played little, other than that.

Because colleges could sign as many players as they wished, every team in the SEC fielded a freshman football team with a three game schedule. We played Vanderbilt, LSU, and Mississippi State every year.

Unbelievably, I also played on the freshman team, which competed on Friday afternoons. In 1953, we played Vandy Friday afternoon in Hemingway. At 6:00 p.m., Marvin Trauth, a former varsity tackle, then a student coach, and I, drove all night to Baton Rouge (on two-lane roads), arriving at 7:00 the following morning. That night I kicked off to start the game against L.S.U.

Anyway, in 1953, Mississippi State's football team revolved around an All-American center/linebacker from Eupora, Cubby Easterwood.

Cubby, later to become a friend, earned his All-American selection with vicious tackles on defense and relentless blocks on offense, along with his over-all aggressiveness.

On kick-offs, the muscular Bulldog lined up directly in front of the kicker. While the kicker was running toward the teed ball, we saw on the film of State's games that year, Easterwood ran toward the kicker. By the time the kicker brought his kicking leg back to the ground and gained some degree of bodily control, Cubby would have gotten to him – more quickly than anyone I had ever seen – usually with a body block into the knees at the end of a full-speed sprint. He had sent several kickers hobbling to the sidelines that year.

I was concerned – even before the student manager brought me the message on Monday afternoon before the State game on Saturday.

"Unca' Bus (my nickname), Coach Vaught wants to see you."

"Now?"

"Yep, right now."

I was dressing for practice. I walked worriedly into his office clad in my hip pads and football pants. My Uncle Buster Poole was there. He and Coach Vaught were sitting down.

"Coach, you want to see me?" I asked cautiously.

"Yes, sit down for a minute."

I had never been asked to sit down for a talk with my Coach before. I suspected the worst. I was right.

"Paige, Easterwood is the key to both the State offense and defense. Without him, State will be a much less potent team!"

"Yes, Sir?"

"You've seen in the film how he attacks the kicker."

"Yes, SIR!"

"Every kicker he's played against this year has tried to fake him, to evade him."

"Yes, SIR!"

"We don't want you to do that."

"You don't?"

"No. We want YOU to attack HIM."

"Attack him?"

"Yes. He won't be expecting it. Instead of trying to get

around him, we want you to drop a shoulder into him if he comes in high. If he comes in low, pop a knee into his side. You'll surprise him. He may not be able to finish the game."

Buster smiled. "Paige, you're a freshman and about all you do for us is kick off. We want you to greet Easterwood with a big, unexpected welcome, and we want him left lying there. To be honest with you, we're willing to sacrifice you in order to get him."

"You are?"

My uncle laughed. I don't think he really meant it.

"We'll practice it this week," Coach Vaught concluded. "See you on the field."

For four days, Coach Vaught lined them up in front of me after practice, five or six football players whose sole responsibilities were to "Cubby Easterwood" me, throw their mad bodies into my nervous one immediately after I kicked the ball. I was supposed to leave them lying where they fell. By Saturday, I had ignorantly convinced myself I could do it, despite my multiple bruises.

We won the toss, and like Coach Vaught so often did, elected to kick. When I raised my head after placing the ball on the tee, I looked straight into the eyes of the All-American. I thought I saw a sneer. I tried to keep from being distracted. It was hard.

"Keep your head down, Paige," I counseled myself, "Don't be afraid! Easterwood is no tougher than the guys you've been hitting all week. Also, don't lie to yourself–! Oh, what the hell – just kick the ball!"

The ball felt solid against my toe and my right leg extended high into the air as my body left the ground. The roar of the crowd, so loud to me when I placed the ball on the kicking tee, dissolved in the surge of concern about my assignment.

Could an All-American hit me harder than my team-mates?

Well, hell, I guess so! He's an All-American!

Did the outcome of the game depend upon me?

Well, hell, I guess so! That's what Coach Vaught said!

Was I up to the task?

Well, hell, I guess so! Maybe! I don't know!

Would Buster kill me if I failed?

Well–well-YEP!

My left foot, which had been pulled off the ground by the thrust of my kicking leg, had barely settled back to earth, when I jerked my head up. Cubby, ten yards away, was sprinting straight at me. I quickly brought my right leg back to the ground. Now he was five yards away. I could hear him breathing hard as he prepared to hit me – and I could see the fire in his eyes. Still only at half speed, I moved directly toward him.

"He's coming in high," I thought. Two yards away I faked as though I would try to evade him to his right, causing him to raise his head and shoulders slightly. I dropped my right shoulder and slammed it hard into his chest. I surprised him and he grunted as his solid body recoiled off my shoul-der and crashed against the ground. I sprang over his pros-trate form with exuberance and dashed quickly downfield toward the ball-carrier, who had caught my kickoff some-where around the goal line.

"I did it – I did it – I can't believe I did it – but I did it!"

State had apparently called a middle return because the runner headed straight up the field toward me. No one else blocked me and the kick-off returner and I were quickly closing the interval between us as we both sprinted directly toward each other. When the gap shrunk to about ten yards, I slowed down, spread my legs, for control, and prepared to make the tackle. I wondered why the ball-carrier, still running at full speed, exhibited no apparent interest in the fact that I was about to hit him.

I didn't wonder long!

I never saw the block, from my right side, coming. Suddenly, my cleats sprang free of the turf, and both of my assaulted legs flew high into the crisp autumn air. When the ball-carrier sailed by me, my airborne feet swung above his head and my astonished eyes gazed futilely at his pumping knees.

I crashed helplessly, like a loblolly pine tree in the midst of a Mississippi tornado, into a heap directly upon my adversary, who with his arms and legs, vigorously pushed me off. When finally we became disentangled, my helmeted head lay no more than 24 inches from his. A big, bulldog grin spread across his satisfied face. Then, lifting himself onto one elbow, he winked at me and said, "Gotcha, Freshman!"

It was Easterwood.

I wanted to ask him how he did that, but by then, I could only think about Buster. He met me ten yards out on the field.

"Well, you CERTAINLY knocked th' hell out of him, Paige! What were y'all doing out there – brother-in-lawing?"

I knew better than to answer.

The game ended in a 7-7 tie.

YOU GONNA KILL THE GRASS

In case you ever wondered what the red-shirt and

freshmen football players did when the varsity played games away from home during the Nineteen Forties and Fifties, this story will explain it. They scrimmaged – full game contact, kicking and all, under the direction of Wobble.

"Y'all were playing off somewhere," Gayle (Tar-Baby) Bowman remembered to Gene Dubuisson and me at Dock-of-the-Bay Restaurant in Bay St. Louis where we enjoyed lunch one day, "so we had our usual hellacious game-scrimmage. Jackie Simpson and I were freshmen and the red-shirts were punting. I was returning the punt to the right."

A right-return punt meant that the returning linemen would hold their opponents at the line of scrimmage until the ball was kicked. Then they would retreat back in the direction of the punt-returner, forming a lane on the right sideline by blocking the players covering the punt in–toward the middle of the field.

"The red-shirts had a big tackle named Jerry. He was Simpson's man. Rock had to block him in. I caught the punt and started up the middle of the field to make the tacklers think it was a middle return. Then I cut toward the right sideline and my lane."

Gayle saw big Jerry lumbering up the middle of the field. Then, he spotted Simpson, peeling off, heading toward Jerry. Simpson and Jerry were both running full speed when the freshman popped his shoulder into the side of the red-shirt's head.

"Jerry looked like a big pine tree falling," laughed Tar-Baby. "He was lying on the ground face down when I went by and hadn't moved a muscle."

Tar-Baby ran on down the sideline and scored.

"I jogged back up the field after scoring," the freshman remembered, "and we were getting ready to kick off when I noticed Jerry still layin' face down where he fell. He still hadn't budged."

Someone yelled, "Coach, Jerry still hasn't moved!"

Wobble, who was huddling with the kick-off team, glanced over toward the wounded warrior, then strolled over to where he lay. Gazing down into the back of the huge tackle's helmeted head, he nudged him with his foot. Then with considerable anxiety oozing from his voice, the concerned Coach exhorted, "Jerry, you roll over ever now and then, you hear? – so you don't kill the grass."

HOW DO YOU KNOW?

If you read *Walk Carefully Around the Dead* you recognized the fact that the great preponderance of players who played at Ole Miss in the late Forties, Fifties, and early Sixties both feared and respected our coaches, especially Wobble. He possessed the unique ability to levy the harshest penalty upon us for our misdeeds and then have us laughing about it before bedtime that night. His one-liners, as discussed, came to be known as Wobbleisms and will live for as long as Rebel football exists, those sententious statements uttered suddenly without forethought. Every player from the aforementioned years remembers at least one and most of us can recall many. And so it was with Warner Alford, former player and esteemed Athletic Director at Ole Miss in the 1980's and early 1990's.

Warner was a freshman in 1956, my senior year. He still recalls vividly one of Wobble's unforgettable utterances on the football field.

"It was early in my freshman year," reminisced Warner, "and the freshmen went 'down under.' " (The Freshmen practiced directly behind the stadium on the property where a parking lot now lies. "Down under" was the field upon which the varsity practiced, directly west of the freshman practice field and fifteen feet lower. "Down under" represented much more than geography, however, it described the ominous journey of the freshmen down the embankment to scrimmage the varsity. It was a gut-check, a tempering of first-year mettle, a severe testing of nerve and no freshman ever entered that arena indifferently.)

"The scrimmage was furious," continued Warner, "and the hitting was violent. The freshmen were making a pretty good showing and Wobble was freely substituting, giving every freshman a chance to prove what he could do."

Finally toward the end of the scrimmage, the freshman coach put a very nervous guard into the fray, on defense. The varsity ran a play directly at him and the newcomer ended up on the bottom of a very large pile of human flesh.

"I can't remember his name but I remember what he said," reviewed Alford. "From beneath the heap he yelled at the top of his lungs, 'Coach, Coach, my leg is broke, my leg is broke.' As each player extricated himself from the stack the frantic worrier would scream again. Coach Wobble casually glanced toward the mass of humanity until finally all the players except the 'injured' freshman stood up-right, at which time he shrieked again, 'Coach, Coach, my leg is broke, my leg is broke.'"

Wobble, now standing directly over the prostrate player, looked sternly down into his anguished face, gazing disdainfully at him for a full 30 seconds. Finally the coach responded.

"How in hell do you know your leg is broken, you're not a doctor. Get your ass off the ground."

With that the stricken guard pushed himself off the turf, re-assumed his defensive stance and practiced the rest of the day. Dr. Wobble had once again correctly diagnosed the "injury."

LET HIM RUN

Ole Miss played Mississippi State in Starkville the last regular season game of 1955. With a victory that day we would win the SEC and be invited to the Cotton Bowl to play the Southwest Conference Champions, TCU. We did – and we were!

State featured a great All-American running back from Clarksdale, Art Davis. For two weeks we worked on a defense designed to control him. We didn't know he had gotten hurt in a game before ours and would not play against us – that is, would not play but one play.

Bobby Fisher, our left end, remembers, "We were ahead of State pretty good in the last quarter (it was 26-0) and Art hadn't played. We didn't know why. State had the ball and we were in our defensive huddle when we heard the State fans suddenly roar. Art was limping onto the field."

Our left tackle, playing next to Bobby, was Richard Weiss from Clarksdale, Art's best friend. Richard pleaded, "Fellows, Art must be hurt pretty bad. Why don't we just let him run?"

A mild argument ensued but finally we reluctantly agreed to let him run. "Don't let him score, though," someone warned. "Tackle him before he scores."

The ball was on State's 40-yard line. Art took the ball on a sweep around his left end.

"We all just kinda hit the offensive linemen," Bobby recalled, "and fell to the ground. Art cleared our line and suddenly got into our secondary, where some of our defensive secondary missed him on purpose."

Buster Poole, our defensive coach, was going wild on the sideline.

Art was running wild on the field.

Finally, we tackled him on about our twenty-five yard line after he had criss-crossed the field through the midst of deliberately missed tackles.

Art pushed himself off the ground and limped to the sideline. With that one run Art gained more yardage than the rest of the State team for the entire day.

We kept State from scoring and the game ended 26-0. Before we left the stadium, the Cotton Bowl invitation was extended and accepted.

Fisher's uncle had come to the game and Bobby rode with him back to Lexington, his home town, for the weekend.

"By the time I showered and dressed and we got to Lexington, all the State and Ole Miss fans had made it back and were congregated at the local sports meeting place, the drugstore. We stopped by–."

When Bobby walked in, the fellows patted him on the back and congratulated him for the win and the Cotton Bowl invitation. One of his best friends, John Stuart Watson, a big State fan, was in the crowd.

"John Stuart was a great State fan," Bobby explained. "He really loved State and he loved football."

After all the accolades had died down, John Stuart got Bobby by the arm and pulled him away from the crowd. Almost whispering, he declared, "Bobby, I'm really proud of you and Ole Miss has had a great year but did you see ol' Art when they finally put him in the ball game? He didn't play but one play and he ran all over the field on y'all. I think we would have won if they had left him in the game!!"

"Bobby," I asked him when he told me the story, "did you ever tell him differently?"

"No, I just let him believe it."

Forty-three years later, Richard Weiss and I walked into the bank in Clarksdale where Art, at this writing, works. Spotting us through his open office door, Art yelled across the entire bank floor over the heads of six tellers and ten customers, "Paige Cothren, the only man who ever caught me from behind."

I shouted back, "Art, your broken leg equalized our speed."

In reviewing the State game film while preparing for the Cotton Bowl, Buster sneered, "In all my days of coaching that was the worst exhibition of tackling I have ever seen!"

I lacked the courage to tell him–!!

FIRST BASE?

One of college sports' greatest changes in these latter years lies in the area of recruiting. In the late Forties, Fifties, and early Sixties, colleges could recruit as many football players as their "plates" could hold. Ole Miss was no exception. Ninety-two players trotted out on the freshman football field my first year, the fall of 1953. There wasn't a bad player in the bunch.

All Ole Miss fans over forty will remember the glorious pre-NCAA-power days when Rebel athletes signed to play football could also play other sports. Eddie Crawford, (1953-1957) present Ole Miss Athletic Director, played football, basketball, and baseball, the last Rebel football player to play all three "major" sports.

For part of the 1941 basketball season, five Pooles, all relatives, started for the Rebels. They all came to Ole Miss on football scholarships.

The man most responsible for securing multi-talented players for Ole Miss was head football scout and head baseball coach, Tom Swayze. So adept was he at finding these talented athletes, he often received jesting derision from the football coaches. "Hell, Tom, we all know the reason you signed that guy! He's a good baseball player!"

Such was the luxury of unlimited football scholarships. Not every football coach was completely pleased with the scouting tactic, however, because not every coach was a baseball fan. Wobble Davidson respected baseball players, shall we say carefully, somewhat less than he did football players. Most of the time he controlled his disposition of mind – occasionally he didn't.

One day in freshman football practice, a player named Carl was rendered semi-conscious. He wasn't completely out, so Wobble was trying to help him "clear his mind." Carl lay prostrate upon the ground. Wobble leaned over him, one hand on his own knee, one grasping Carl's helmet, vigorously shaking the fallen athlete's groggy head.

"Boy, what's your name?"

"Carl."

"Where are you?"

"Ole Miss."

"What position do you play?"

"First base."

As quickly as the coach had attempted to revive the stricken warrior, he rose from over him with measured disgust.

No one quite heard his garbled comment, but the tone of his voice was unmistakable.

AIN'T GONNA BE NO COMEBACK!

In 1952, Ole Miss earned one of its greatest football victories. The Rebels beat the number one team in the nation, Maryland, 14-7 at Oxford. The next year we played the Terps at Maryland. I was a Freshman, playing on the varsity.

Maryland was mad!!

They were also loaded with All-Americans – four. I later played with one of them, Ron Waller, in Los Angeles. Another Maryland consensus All-American was "Little Mo" Mojeleski, a huge tackle, and the best college lineman in America that year.

Ole Miss had been decimated by graduation the previous spring. Jimmy "King" Lear, the Reb's All-American quarterback, was gone along with almost all of the starters who had defeated the Terps the year before. The team consisted of mostly sophomores, a few juniors and a few seniors.

On the flight to Washington the day before the game, Henry Linton, a starting tackle and the team jester, somehow enticed a flight attendant to let him man the intercom system. He clowned almost the entire trip from his newly acquired podium, declaring among other things, that we were going to beat Maryland again.

Not only was Maryland mad, but they were very mad, and determined to rectify the disaster of the previous year.

Early in the game, the ball was placed on the right hash-mark directly in front of the Ole Miss bench. Ole Miss had the ball. Henry, playing in front of Little Mo, popped him on the chin with a wicked forearm, knocking him out.

"He was lying on the field right in front of our bench," Bobby Fisher remembered, "and a time-out was called. The Maryland trainers finally revived him and got him up on his feet, smelling salts under his nose, wiping his face with cold towels. So we all go to hollering at the All-American – 'Get up, you big Son of a B—h, you sissy, get up.'"

Little Mo, now partially awake, looked at the Ole Miss bench, scowled, reached down and jerked his helmet off the ground and slammed it onto his disoriented head. Glaring at the jeering Ole Miss sideline, over his shoulder, he stumbled with the help of the trainer to the Maryland bench. A few plays later, fully revived, he jogged back onto the field.

"When he came back on the field," Bobby continued, "we were all watching him, 'cause we figured there would be some action. Sure enough, there was!"

The very next play Little Mo came from the ground with a right fist and caught Henry under the chin. Linton's head snapped back, his eyes rolled back in his head, his feet left the ground and he crashed to the earth, out cold. A minute later, Henry still hadn't moved, so Doc Knight called for a stretcher and two managers carried the torpid tackle into the dressing room.

By half-time, the Terps led us 28-0, and had pounded us physically. Depressed and bewildered, the Rebs silently marched into the dressing room. No-one said a word, the overwhelming quiet displaying our stupor-like spirits.

Henry still lay comatose on his canvas couch.

With about three minutes left in the halftime break, Buster Poole, my uncle and our defensive coach, decided he would try to stimulate our benumbed emotions with a dynamic fire and brimstone sermon. "We can still win this game, men, all we need to do is come off the snap of the ball with some aggression – put a shoulder pad to them, fellows, let's get going – we can COMEBACK—!

The word "COMEBACK" somehow filtered its way into Henry's inert brain, causing his body to quiver slightly. Rising up from his portable casket on one elbow, his eyes rolled back in his head, and with a thick tongue, he loudly affirmed – "I AIN'T GONNA COMEBACK!!"

He wasn't the only one. The Terps won 39-0.

The trip home was twice as long as the one up there – and no player dared engage the public address system.

STAND UP, JOE

It was a hot September Friday in Oxford and the Ole Miss freshman team had just lost a heart breaker to LSU, 28 to 21. Freshman Coach Wobble was incensed at the way his team had played. He collected the players for a meeting in the dressing room. Some of them were sprawled out on the floor, trying to stretch the cramps out of their salt-depleted arms and legs. Some sat on the benches in front of their lockers, their heads hanging in dejection and disappointment and perhaps fear of forthcoming reprisal, their elbows resting upon their knees, supporting bodies heaving in shortness of breath. Others, who played little that day sat on the dressing room bleachers. Sweat tumbled from all of them, forming for each athlete his own small liquid pool on the tiled floor. No one talked loudly and few at all, except an occasional whisper as though the Rebel dressing room had mutated into a funeral parlor.

Wobble appeared suddenly in their midst. Every head and every eye turned toward the distraught coach, disgust written upon his face. You could have heard the proverbial pin drop.

"We knew the next week was gonna be bad," Worthy McClure and Richard Smith remembered. "The varsity players on their way past our dressing room out to practice said so – filing by, smiling, and shaking their heads. Coach Wobble confirmed it."

"Well, little girls, I want you to go home to your mamas this weekend, and if you want to live, you might ought to

STAY THERE."

Then the irate leader turned and walked briskly from the room.

"Many of our parents came to the game," Worthy continued, "so we took Coach Wobble at his word and went home. We dared to hope it wasn't the last time."

In those days, a Southern airline flight from Jackson to Oxford cost only $12.00, so four players flew back – Worthy, Randy Reed, Riley Myers, and Joe Jordan.

Joe Jordan lived in Meadeville, but he had grown up in Louisiana. He moved to the Mississippi town for his last year of high school when he became too old to play in the Pelican State. He was a very quiet, reserved, but older freshman.

"The four of us got on the plane and sat facing each other. Randy, Riley, and I moaned about how bad the week was gonna be, all the way to Oxford," mused Worthy, "but Joe didn't say a word – all the way to Oxford – he never said a word. He just looked at us, never smiling. We told every horror story we could imagine, how bad it was gonna be – !"

When the four of them returned to the athletic dorm on Sunday night, several varsity players met them in the lobby with bad news – "Y'all are gonna die tomorrow." Joe said nothing.

The next afternoon before practice, the managers assembled the football team in the locker room for a meeting – a few minutes later, Wobble entered the room.

"Well, ladies, I see you decided to come back. I've been thinking about the team all weekend while you were visiting your mamas. A team this terrible made me try to find out who recruited you. "Hell, I've talked to Swayze and the other coaches, and I can't find anybody who'll take credit for recruiting any of you except one man – Joe Jordan, the only football

139

player in this room – the only one who played worth a s–t Friday, the only one on this entire team with guts – the ONLY ONE. JOE, I WANT YOU TO STAND UP so these gutless wonders can take a good look at a football player."

No one moved.

"Joe, STAND UP!"

Still, no one stirred.

"Joe, STAND UP, MAN, I'm proud of you!"

Silence and stillness! The other players looked around the room.

"Joe? Where are you?"

Thirty seconds later, a reticent voice from the crowd, Ernie Brown from Biloxi murmured, "Coach, he quit and went home."

THE BADDEST WEEK THERE EVER WAS – !

Writing books like *Walk Carefully Around the Dead* and this one furnishes the writer with countless moments of enjoyment, provided by the interviews with old comrades, teammates, and friends. As these old warriors recall and tell ancient stories, memories get jogged and laughter ensues. Such was the visit with Joe Pasley, presently of Oxford, and long-time director of Camp Lake Stephens, a Methodist retreat just a few miles out of town on the old Pontotoc Road. I called Joe to set up the interview. I hadn't seen him in several years. We were freshmen together.

"Joe?"

"Yes?"

"This is Paige – Paige Cothren."

"Unca' Bus! – how you doin'?"

140

"Fine – and you?"

"Great. What can I do for you?"

"I need to talk to you."

"You want to repent, huh?" he kidded (I think).

"Ah, well, kinda," I laughed, "repent for not having interviewed you for the book I'm writing."

"You're writing another book?"

"Yeah. I know you have some old stories and I need to interview a Pasley. I tried to talk to that turkey brother of yours too, but I could never pin him down. When can you see me?" (Brother Lea who lives in Tupelo.)

"Where are you?" he asked.

"Memphis."

"Can you come to Oxford this afternoon?"

"Sure can."

"I'll meet you at McDonalds – 3 o'clock."

"In Oxford?"

"Yes – the one on University, across from Big Star."

* * * * *

"I have two stories I want to tell you, Paige, but one of them is about you."

"Make me look good or bad?"

"No way it can make you look good 'less it's fiction. Makes you look, well, kinda rural."

"And the other story?" I asked Joe.

"THAT one makes ME look crazy – or at least explains why I am! Which one you want me to tell first?"

I looked around to see if anyone was sitting close

enough to hear before I answered, unenthusiastically, "Let's get me out of the way."

"You remember how afraid of flying you were back then?"

"No way I could forget, José."

You remember our flight to Biloxi after Christmas to practice for the Sugar Bowl?"

"I try not to – thanks for reminding me. What do you remember about it – and me?"

Joe broke into a wide grin and I surmised he had told the story many times. He seemed more anxious to tell the story than I was to hear it, and with fractured confidence I relented. "Go ahead and make me look bad, Joe."

"I remember how scared of flying you were and starting a week before we flew to games that entire year, you would ask Doc Knight (our Trainer) five million questions. 'What time we leaving now, Doc? How high we gonna be flying? How long will it take us to get there? Will we land on a long runway?', etc., etc., etc."

"Wonder why I asked DOC all those questions?"

"Probably because he said the prayers before games."

"Yeah, that's right – probably."

"Anyway," Joe continued, "when we started to land at Keesler Field in Biloxi, the pilot overshot the runway. You were already 'scrunched' down in your seat. When the pilot shot the power to the plane and pulled it up sharply, you started yelling 'Doc, Doc, Doc, Doc!' By the time we landed you were so low in the seat, the seat belt was around your neck and you were still calling for Doc."

Joe was laughing vigorously by the time he finished the tale and I had to pull him out from under the McDonald's table.   In his endeavor to illustrate my slide, he affected one of his own. I regained some dignity.

"Well, that was really funny, Joe" with tongue in cheek I surmised, "but now I want to hear the one which makes you look crazy. I think I'll enjoy that one more."

" 'Spect you will. 'Cause I'm gonna' tell you about the baddest week there ever was – at least for me."

"What happened to you?"

"I guess you don't remember, then?"

"Maybe I will after I hear about it again," I declared, with a little embarrassment. I recognized a touch of hurt in him.

"It started on Tuesday, before we played Tennessee on Saturday, Paige. I was on the red-shirt team and we were running the single-wing against y'all. I was playing tailback–."

"Johnny Majors," I interrupted.

"Yeah," Joe laughed. "I was Johnny Majors. Anyway, I ran a tailback sweep and when I got to the sideline, instead of just goin' on out of bounds like I should have, I cut back and all eleven of y'all hit me, I think. Knocked me coo coo. When I came to, Doc Knight was leaning over me and I heard him say 'he's cut his lip off.' My teeth had stuck out through my lip, blood was everywhere."

The doctor stitched Joe's lip back together an hour later. A couple of hours after that, he fully revived.

"Then on Thursday afternoon," Joe continued, "I was standing down on one end of the practice field with the rest of the red-shirts. We were crowded around Wobble, looking at a play in his notebook and I had taken my helmet off, which we were allowed to do occasionally. The second and third teams were running pass plays on the other end of the field and Houston Patton, who could throw the football five miles, let loose a long one. It hit me right on top of the head."

Joe bit the dust again, out cold.

"Paige, you remember on Fridays, before football games on Saturdays, the red-shirts and freshmen would scrimmage, game conditions?"

"Yes."

"Well, I was a red-shirt and we were scrimmaging the freshmen. I was playing linebacker. On a sweep, a freshman clipped me from behind and Monroe Pointer's helmet hit me flush in the face as I was falling. Knocked me out again. Three times in one week.

"Dang, Joe, did anybody ever take you to the doctor?"

"Naw, you remember how it was back then!"

"Yeah."

"But for the next two weeks I had a major problem."

"What was that, Joe?"

"Well, you remember a bell rang on the campus to start classes and end classes."

"Yeah."

"Man, for two weeks I went to classes I didn't even have!"

CHAPTER VIII

TO BE INITIATED

Many events experienced by athletes at Ole Miss in the late forties, fifties, and early sixties were extremely funny. Those episodes compelled me to write both *Walk Carefully Around the Dead* and this book. Hopefully, to some degree, they amuse everyone who reads them.

As in all of society, some deeds might have delighted one group of people but provoked others. Archie Bunker illustrates that possibility.

A few incidents, however, were so terrible that they cheered no one either at the time they occurred or now – Archie Manning's broken arm, for example.

One activity executed upon every Ole Miss athlete, though, fits none of the three categories.

The M-Club Initiation.

Through the intervening years, since I stumbled from the Ole Miss Field House following my astonishing survival of the occurrence, I have sought one word by which the initiation might be defined. I consulted my dictionary. The word wasn't there.

I enlisted the experiential aid of many athletes who, like me, endured it. Their composite comment was, "Hell, Paige, you might as well not write about the initiation – no one's gonna believe it!" so they failed to help me.

Finally, I desperately searched through my trusty Synonym Finder, a very thick book which contains all the words in the King's English, even those altered by American slang, and their synonyms. That intellectual quest failed, too.

I've decided no one word exists by which the M-Club initiation of the forties, fifties, and perhaps early sixties might be explained. In fact, I've concluded there are no combination of words, no stringing together of graphic expressions, no listing of colorful phrases to illustrate it accurately.

Inherent within the torturous experience lies a true dichotomy. The initiation generated inordinate fear in its inductees, while providing utmost satisfaction later for having endured it. It spawned an inexpressible anger while fostering a profound companionship with the persecutors who engendered the anger; it effected pride and honor in an environment of shame, a proud ship maneuvering through an ocean of storms – a lonely agony which few chose to evade – an ecstacy which the oppressed shared with the oppressors. And when old lettermen congregate, they verbally dissect it – they frown, they wince, they smile, they groan, they laugh and they wonder, often out loud, "Why in hell did I ever go through THAT?"

THAT TERRIBLE SUNDAY NIGHT

I started worrying about the initiation mid-way through my first lettering season, my sophomore year. I quickly discovered worrying about it didn't help, but it didn't seem to hurt anything either. The agony would be the same regardless.

I thought about blaming a couple of my fumbles on the anticipation of it but figured our coaches were too smart to accept THAT. I could hear Uncle Bus' comment, "You fumble again, Nephew, you're gonna sprint into that initiation to avoid me."

For a while, I envisioned that playing really good games might encourage the older players, the M-Club members, to soften a little, carrying more than my own load, you know, but as the time of suffering grew closer, I realized the veterans weren't any more impressed with me, a starter, than with the players who barely lettered. Besides, Slick McCool, who lettered the year before, and I, both played fullback.

Then I imagined the veterans might ease up on me a little because I was Coach Buster's nephew. Under closer scrutiny that theory dissolved for two reasons: I heard Buster laughing about the upcoming initiation; and I remembered how tough he had been on all the players. My groping mind neither assuaged my fears nor produced comfort.

Along with all the other new lettermen, I waited in absolute apprehension for the "big show," Sunday night, eleven o'clock following the 1955 Sugar Bowl game. I wondered if our Mamas knew what was gonna happen to their sons. No, probably not – otherwise they would be speeding toward Oxford.

In 1954, Ole Miss won 9 games and lost 2, one of them to Navy in the ensuing Sugar Bowl, a game which we had been expected to win by a wide margin. Our coaches were not happy – and the old lettermen were angry. Sunday night would come all too soon.

I thought about running away!

An M-Club meeting was called for Sunday afternoon and new lettermen were required to attend. The President of the M-Club presided. Fear probably caused me to forget who he was – George Harris perhaps — I'll never forget what he said.

"Be in the hallway immediately outside the M-Club room at 11 o'clock tonight. For the sake of your big asses, you'd better not be late. You'll be smart to wear only blue jeans, no underwear. Bring a towel. Have two or three freshmen meet you in your rooms about 1:30 a.m. And new lettermen, we older players hope you enjoy this night as much as we will – heh, heh, heh."

I recruited two freshmen, Don Fritchi and Bobby Posegay, both from Slidell, Louisiana. They were not happy with their disconsolate team-mate. I was too concerned about me to care!

If the beleaguered bunch of new lettermen were nervous walking to the dorm after the meeting, we were doubly fearful walking back to the old gym, the location of the M-Club room, late that night. Most of us were barefooted and wore only blue jeans. A few fellows wore t-shirts, several others shoes. I don't remember anyone saying anything on the way, although I imagine we were all thinking the same uncomfortable thoughts.

We arrived before 11 o'clock and were herded up against the wall outside the M-Club room, holding our towels and trying to hide the anticipation which must have flashed across our faces.

My heart sounded like a woodpecker thrusting his beak against a hollow oak tree. Sweat cascaded down my flushed face and body, defying the cold midnight air of January, in which we had to walk to get there. I tried to look confident, with no confidence, bold with little courage. I wanted to run, to escape. I knew, perhaps better than the others, what lay before us, having heard my three uncles and five cousins who had already lettered, talk about it. "No," I thought weakly, "I won't be the first football player to evade the initiation," as badly as I want to–!

The cool wall was moist against my perspiring back as I searched the faces of my older teammates for compassion. Some of them fashioned huge smiles, seeming to anticipate the coming attraction with glee. Some appeared serious, as if THEY were about to endure the initiation, reliving it within the depths of their own minds. Some looked apathetic, indifferent, nonchalant. I found no apparent compassion in any of them.

My concern intensified.

I had hustled down to the gym and up the stairs to the hallway outside the M-Club room for a reason. I wanted to be first in line, so I worked my way through the quickly gathering crowd to a position just outside the door. I knew what "he" was about to do to me, and I wanted it done quickly.

The "he" was Slick McCool.

Bobby "Slick" McCool, from Cleveland, Mississippi, one of the most talented running backs to ever enlist at Ole Miss, was for his day, an offensive warhorse. At 5'11" tall and 210 pounds, he ran like the wind, a ten-flat hundred. His two massive, muscular legs were two brown, carved stones on a Greek statue. He ran over tacklers as well as he ran away from them. He had been chosen as Pre-season All American by several publications.

Slick and I played the same position, although offensively, he played it much better than I, but he suffered the misfortune of arriving to college football the same year the NCAA eliminated two-platoon. That meant Slick would be forced to play defense, not his most potent attribute. Nor could he block with the same devastation as he ran the football, a necessity in Coach Vaught's offensive scheme. Because I could block and play defense a little better, added to that my place-kicking, by mid-season the Herculean runner had been demoted to second string, and I had become the starting fullback. Slick was mad.

"Oh, oh, I'm in trouble now," I moaned to Jerry McKaskel, my roommate. "Slick's gonna kill me in the initiation." He agreed.

Much to my dismay, I soon discovered we were right.

"You're mine in the initiation, Paige, – my meat. I'm

gonna get the first lick on you at the M-Club door, and I'm gonna air mail your ass, - gonna put your head up against the other wall," meaning the wall on the other side of the room.

Being knocked through the M-Club doorway introduced two hours of traumatic episodes, which comprised the M-Club initiation, the first event. Blindfolded with our own towels taped around our heads, we would be told to strip naked; made to bend over in the M-Club doorway; and with unique and abhorrent accommodation, "welcomed" into the organization – via a baseball bat shaved down into a 2-inch paddle, swung as hard as, in my case, an angry, disgruntled ex-starting fullback could swing it. The last guy to shed his clothing enjoyed the privilege of joining twice.

I knew Slick, regardless of what I did or said, good or bad, was going to hit me as hard as he could. Since the initiation itself would strip all pride and dignity from me, I assumed, albeit temporarily, an arrogant attitude.

"No, you aren't gonna air-mail me, Slick, and you aren't gonna put my head against the other wall." I secretly wished the rest of my head could be as confident as my mouth.

"Yeah, smart ass, I'm gonna put your head against the other wall."

* * * * *

"Well, here I am, smart ass! You wanna' bet I don't air mail your butt up against the other wall? You confident enough to put some money on it?"

I was still propped against the wall, dampened by the sweat of fear and nervousness. Slick stood directly in front of me, his emboldened eyes flashing into my glazed ones.

I didn't answer. My throat was too tight and dry.

"That's what I thought! You're not so tough right now, are you, smart ass?"

I knew I had to answer him.

He folded my towel around my head and started tap-ing it.

With all the false courage I could convene, trepidation probably elevating my voice an octave higher, I squeaked, "No, you aren't gonna air-mail me up against the other wall, Slick."

He laughed!

"Pull 'em off," a loud veteran's voice from somewhere in the crowd commanded.

A second later I stood naked before the jeering horde of teammates. One of the inductees, I can't remember who, won the double-lick honor. He had worn shoes and a t-shirt, I later discovered.

"At least I avoided one lick," I thought. Before the night ended, I would discover it didn't matter.

Slick grabbed me by the arm. "Let's go, smart ass."

I knew he was leading me the ten feet or so to the M-Club doorway. I tried to elevate myself into psychological preparedness, but the woodpecker intensified his rhythmic beating.

"If this ten foot walk is a microcosm of a walk to the electric chair," I thought, "Mother will never have to worry about me committing a major crime."

I thought I knew what Slick would do. He would get a running start, so I figured just about the time the baseball bat approached my rear, I would lean backward. That ought to shift the balance of my weight, offset the force of the blow some, and keep me earthbound. The slight increase in pain, I thought, would be incidental.

"Grab your ankles, smart ass," Slick bellowed.

"Oh, oh," I thought, "I can't lean back holding my ankles."

Slick must have pulled his shoes off. Even on the tile floor I never heard him coming, but I had no trouble hearing one sound – the message of board against flesh – even before the voice of pain reached the ears of my posterior, the lick from Slick apparently deadening the nerves. And I immediately experienced weightlessness as my feet separated from the tile floor. A second later I slid belly down against the wall on the other side of the M-Club room. A second after that, the feeling in my rump resurrected, propelling the pain throughout my body. My frustration from losing the contest didn't help.

"I told you, smart-ass!"

I lay on the cool tile floor wondering if its temperature might moderate the pain. I felt my butt. It was red-hot. "No," I reasoned, "it's too sensitive to sit on–!" I wondered if it was bleeding, but blind-folded, I couldn't really tell. "Probably better," I thought.

"Get out of the way, Cothren," I heard a harsh voice yell, "we've got some more heads to put up against the wall." I crawled to my right until another wall stopped me.

"Grab your ankles," resounding voices demanded every ten seconds or so, followed by the sharp crack of wood against flesh, effecting boisterous laughter and unsympathetic evaluations.

"Wow, way to swing!"

"Now THAT'S what I call a RED ass!"

"I believe you drew a little blood!"

"So far Slick's got the hardest lick."

I wondered if I was supposed to extract some pride

from that!

When all the new lettermen had been "received" into the athletic fraternity, someone yelled, "To the field house." I struggled to stand. Every change in the position of my body seemed to aggravate the nerves in my rear-end. I knew all the other players were experiencing the same trauma, and I questioned my lack of sympathy for them.

Years later in the counseling office, I would learn an important truth. Personal pain prohibits pity!

Slick dug his energized fingers into my quivering biceps and growled, "Let's go." Then he led me across the M-Club room, down the hall, down the stairs and the quarter-mile to the field house on the East end of Hemingway Stadium.

I kept my mouth shut, and I wondered if other students were watching. We were nude.

I shivered in the enveloping cold, and I could hear the other inductees behind me, stumbling, groaning, falling, grunting. We were all too smart to complain, although due not to lack of desire. Lamenting would produce no magnanimity in our tormentors.

I thought about reminding Slick that a mommy "kisses away" the pain of a hurting child. Would he do that for me? That was one of my shortest-lived considerations.

THE REST OF THE STORY

My sense of touch declared that we had been herded into Doc Knight's large taping room. I leaned against one of the tables.

"Now," Slick decreed, "the fun really begins."

I dared to hope he was joking. Reality denied it.

"Y'all are gonna be given a glass full of a great tasting drink," a voice blurted out, "and you've got to swallow it and hold it down for ten seconds. If you puke it up before then, you'll have to try again until you do—.

"What is it?" someone asked. I assumed he was one of the tormented.

"You don't ask US questions, wise-ass, – we ask YOU questions. We're initiating you, remember? Grab your ankles."

A second later I heard a loud "splat." I figured the inquisitor had tasted the baseball bat again. I hurled every question from my mind.

Slick thrust his thick fingernails into my retracting arm muscle again and pulled. "Come on, smart-ass, we're goin' to the shower room."

I could hear the others around me, shuffling in the same direction. Whatever befell me, I knew would be happening to everyone, a thought producing more concern than comfort. "In this case," I concluded, "company lessens little the misery."

The filled glass felt cool against my hand, but the putrid smell wafting from it screamed of decaying flesh, acres of garlic, an uncovered septic tank. I tried in vain to identify it and my anxiety intensified.

"Well, at least it's not poison," I speculated. "The coaches wouldn't let 'em kill us. They would lose half of the football team."

I had never tasted anything remotely close to it. The noxious smell was abominable, the taste ten-thousand times worse.

I had forced about half of the thick mixture down my resisting throat when suddenly a mystic, medicinal demon slammed his heavy fist into my pulsating stomach. The liquid potpourri exploded from my mouth and eased out of my nose. I dropped to my knees and gagged, every muscle in my contracting mid-section cooperating to cast the rancid goulash from my body, against my will.

"Wal', look at the big, tough fullback – can't even hold a little ol' mixed drink down for ten seconds. Fill that boy's glass up again."

I didn't bother to rise off my knees. I closed my eyes, restricted the flow of air through my nostrils, and took a deep breath, released it, turned the glass up and swallowed.

"Thousand one, thousand two, thousand three–," the fist dug into my belly again. Extreme nausea encompassed me. I was determined. I could hear others gagging around me.

"Hold it – hold it – hold it," voices cheered and encouraged.

"Thousand four, thousand five, thousand six –," the nausea increased. My hands pushed against the shower floor, my arms weakening quickly. I tried to close my throat.

"Thousand seven, thousand eight, thousand nine —." Extreme dizziness, absolute vertigo. The strength drained from my enfeebled arms – my lethargic head drooped to the tile. "Hold it, Paige, hold it," I warned myself.

"Thousand ten!"

The lethal libation detonated within my body and burst from my mouth, my nose – an Old Faithful erupting inside of me, casting the foul substance onto the shower floor. I thought I was losing consciousness. I hoped so!!

"Get your ass off the floor, Cothren. You know Uncle Bus wouldn't like you laying on the floor. Get up."

I struggled to my feet, my torpid legs resisting the weight of my listless body. The room whirled a pirouette around my brain. I found the revolving wall and leaned against it.

"Who's the best fullback you ever saw, Cothren?"

The muffled voice drifted from a deep well, slow motion words. It belonged to Slick, and I wanted to give him the right answer. I didn't know what it was!

I partially opened my sluggish eyes, and I felt more vile potion slide from my mouth.

"Kayo Dottley," I thought. I didn't know if that was what Slick wanted to hear. I didn't think so.

"I don't know."

"You don't know? You don't know?! You'd better know."

"Hand me that baseball bat," Slick commanded someone.

I gambled.

"Slick McCool."

"Who? I can't hear you."

"SLICK MCCOOL!"

I was surprised at my volume.

"Wal', how in hell did YOU get to play so much, then, smart-ass?"

"I don't know," I cautiously answered.

"YOU DON'T KNOW? How come you don't know? Reckon Uncle Bus had anything to do with it?"

"No S— ah, ah, YES SIR!"

"Spread your legs, tough guy; you can cover your b–ls

with your hands."

Not only did I cover my private parts with my hands – I tried to cram them up into my soured stomach. They wouldn't go–! I think for the first time in my life, I wanted to be a girl.

For the following hour or so, we were whipped with "stretched out" coat hangers over our entire bodies except our heads and our private parts. The licks were never more than a second or two apart, usually by two or more floggers at a time. At the end of the ordeal, coat hanger cuts covered our bodies.

Finally the beating stopped; the towels were removed from our delirious heads; and our surreal world surrendered its travail. We were sick; we were hurting; we were alive; we were smiling; and the beating had stopped. The worst was over! Our teammates, turned attackers suddenly, had just as quickly become our teammates again. Their cheers and smiles conveyed their respect and comradeship. They seemed to be as glad as we that the severe tribulation had ended. They shook our hands.

I remember thinking, "If you're that happy it's over, why did we have to endure it in the first place?" I quickly and forcefully resisted the temptation to convert that thought into the spoken word.

The same authoritative voice, now recognized, repeated an earlier command. "Spread your legs!"

He continued, "Fellows, this white substance is called plaster-of-paris."

We knew that!! Most of us had already worn it upon members of our bodies to heal bones broken in athletic conflict dating back to our junior high days, and before.

The voice continued, "I know many of you have had

your broken fingers, arms, and legs protected by plaster-of-paris – but Ill bet you've never worn it HERE."

We were "plaster-of-parised" – everywhere our bodies grew hair, except our heads, – our chests, our arms, under our arms, our legs, and our crotches. We were smeared, and patted, and pasted until, for many of us, only the upper parts of our backs, our feet, and our heads were visible, mummies alive, albeit barely, yet grateful.

Finally our tormentors spread newspaper on Doc Knight's floor, and we were positioned upon them. Paint buckets were pried open and the villainous "Van Gogh's" painted their final masterpiece upon our battered bodies – red in front, blue in back, our bodies became loyal manifestations of the Ole Miss Spirit.

"WE'RE THROUGH WITH YOU," the voice exclaimed. "Congratulations. You're now members of the greatest and most exclusive organization in the world – the Ole Miss Rebel M-Club."

My harassed heart failed to elevate to that lofty station. "Thank God it's over!"

The paint stung our coat-hanger cuts, but it could not impel our spirits. A collective yell reverberated off Doc Knight's ceiling, and we started our sluggish yet joyful migration back toward the athletic dorm.

I TRIED to run, but the plaster-of-paris extending from my crotch to my quivering knees, gluing my legs together, restrained me. I must have looked like a penguin moving my legs only from the knees down. After wobbling a hundred yards or so, I stopped near the dark gym where the entire agonizing affair had begun. Taking a deep, doubtful breath, I ripped my plastered legs apart.

Stopping afforded me an opportunity to glance around

at my afflicted comrades. We were the epitome of the motley crew, made similar only by our suffering, our nakedness, and the painted color of our skin. All fifteen or so of us were scattered from the field house to the gym, some halted, feeling their wounds, wondering if any bones were broken; some were walking so slowly I had to gaze upon them intently to determine any movement; some either with less hair or more intestinal fortitude, were jogging as rapidly as they could under the circumstances; some, like me, were wrestling with the adhesive cement which gripped each hair like a dog protecting his favorite bone.

Now freed from part of my concrete confinement, I sprinted, if my movement might be so labeled, toward Garland and my two freshmen who had been given the materials necessary to clean me, and free me.

In January 1999, Warner Alford, former Ole Miss football player and athletic director and I were seated at his kitchen table remembering and laughing about the initiation, probably made funny by the mind-debilitating passage of more than forty years. Warner suffered through the initiation two years after me, with Ralph (Catfish) Smith.

"I still marvel at what Catfish did," mused Warner. "Everyone in my group was ONLY interested in getting back to the dorm and relief. Catfish, who was jogging along side of me said, 'What the hell – as long as I'm this close, I think I'll check my mail,' and he did. Here this figure is, buck naked, plaster-of-paris on all his hairy parts, his body painted red in the front and blue in the back – checking his mail. Must have been SOME sight.!"

"Yeah," I added, "especially if his box was low."

"What in hell happened to you? How are we gonna clean all that off you?" Don asked, as both he and Bobby riveted their dismayed eyes upon me. "And what is that putrid smell? Don't make us do this."

"Where's the turpentine?"

"Right here," one of them answered.

"Where are the rags?"

"Right here."

"Where are the flat razor blades?"

"We have 'em!"

"Freshmen, I don't give a damn if you ARE my friends." (My eyes narrowed.) "I don't care if you lose a whole night's sleep! I don't care if you have to touch my ---- and my ----- getting this plaster-of-paris and paint off me! I don't even care if your entire families and that whole Cajun town you come from get mad at me for making you do it!! CLEAN ME UP AND DO IT QUICK! And don't hurt me. I've used up all my endurance to pain for a while."

The two freshmen looked at one another, then at me. They shook their heads in disbelief and one of them asked, "Do they do this to all lettermen?"

"Your asses will be right here in a year or two. Now get started."

"What do you want us to do first?"

"Get this damn cement off me."

"How do we do that?"

"One hair at a time, and if you CUT me and I DO recover from it, we're gonna have one hell of a freshman meeting."

At 1:30 a.m., the two newly commissioned barbers went to work – at 3:30 they finished.

"Lord, you smell bad," one of the freshmen growled. "Why do you stink so bad?"

"Something they made us drink!"

"What was it?"

"As – asp – asp, something like that. Hell, I don't know! What difference does it make? Get this paint off me, and be careful. They whipped us with coat-hangers and I'm cut all over."

"This turpentine's gonna sting."

"I know – just be careful."

My discontented friends started removing the paint from my tortured torso at 3:30 a.m. They finished at 7:00.

"Do we hafta go to class?" one of them asked.

"I'm not, and I may not go tomorrow. I wouldn't go if I were you. Can you still smell me?"

"Just as bad as ever. You're breathing it out man – it's coming from inside you."

"Go to bed, Freshmen, and thanks. You did a good job."

With sarcasm, Don declared over his shoulder, "Boy, that really makes ME feel good!"

"Watch your mouth. You're still a freshman."

* * * * *

"What was that slop y'all made us drink last night, Eagle?"

It was about 4:00 in the afternoon. I had slept for eight hours and had finally pushed my battered and practically hair-less body out of bed when I heard the quarterback talking loudly. Shuffling barefoot down the hall, I went into his room. Eagle was pulling his letter jacket off.

"Get away from me, Unca' Bus, YOU STINK!"

"What was it?"

"Asfiditty and other stuff."

"What?"

"Asfiditty. You know, the medicine."

"What other stuff?"

"A rotten oyster and chewing tobacco."

"You mean y'all made us drink a glass of this – this – this asfiditty with a rotten oyster and tobacco crumbled up in it? It's a wonder it didn't kill us – and it might yet."

"It ain't gonna kill you Unca' Bus," the quarterback countered. "It just makes you sick and smell bad. Course in your case it probably made you smell better – heh, heh, heh. By the way, I wouldn't ask a girl for a date in person 'til about Friday – not if you really want to go out with her."

"Why not?"

"You'll stink 'til then."

"Eagle, do you remember how important it is for me to block the ends so you can look good running around on game day?"

"Yeah. Why?"

"Don't expect me to block 'em next year."

"Hey, man, as long as Coach Buster is on the sidelines, I'm not worried about you blocking the ends."

Eagle had a point.

* * * * *

Years after my M-Club initiation, I discovered that the "asfiditty" which we drank was asafetida, a "yellow-brown, bitter, malodorous, resinous material derived from the roots of several plants," according to the dictionary. The word "asafetida derives from two words; asa, which translates "gum;" and fetida which means "stinking."

I believe it.

The medicine, seldom used now, was administered for relief of sour stomachs, one drop in an 8-ounce glass of water.

We drank it straight!

It produced fifteen sour stomachs.

CHAPTER IX

THE CONFLICTS WITH COWS

THE RUNAWAY

Not every Poole birthed with the ability to play football at Ole Miss did so. James Swepson "Sonny Boy" Poole, born on the banks of Brushy Creek two years before I came into the world, signed a football scholarship with the Rebels in the Fall of 1951, and reported to Wobble Davidson for practice. My cousin stood 6 feet 2 inches tall, and weighed a very muscular 215 lbs. Had he remained on the training table, he could have comfortably carried 250 lbs., which would have made him one of the largest and fastest linemen in America for his playing years. He would have been a great athlete for Ole Miss.

Sonny Boy chose instead to, as the old-timers phrase it in South Mississippi, "make a doctor." He quit football, entered pre-med, and for more than forty years, practiced medicine in Centreville, less than 20 miles from Homochitto, the Poole ennclave and place of his birth, a mile down the dusty gravel road from Mama Poole's, where Buster, Ray, Barney and I grew up. He became the resident Poole family doctor until his recent retirement and few weeks passed in all those years when he wasn't attending to one of our relatives, either in his clinic or at Field Memorial Hospital nearby.

Sonny Boy's entrance into medicine presented all my other relatives, and me, with an interesting problem. I grew up with him; swam naked with him and all the other Poole boys in the cold, clear, spring-fed waters of Brushy Creek; went to Crosby High with him; and played all three sports with him. To me he's Sonny Boy – then - now - and always. How do you call a Doctor of Medicine, Sonny Boy, especially before other people?

Upon periodically seeing him again, my greeting usually trailed along these lines as I extended my hand. "Hi, Sonny, oh, er, oh, Doc, ah, oh — what the hell, I can't do it. How are you?" I couldn't call him Doctor – he was family! I didn't want to call him Sonny Boy – he was a doctor. In Homochitto, preachers and doctors were practically gods and certainly elevated beyond first-name status. Now that he's retired, I think my conscience will allow me to call him Sonny Boy again. I tried it last Father's Day at Mt. Vernon Methodist Church and it seemed to fit.

Growing up at Homochitto, Sonny Boy's intellectual and academic abilities weren't always recognized, however, not even by the closest of relatives, including his Dad, J. C.

J. C. Poole was one of the few older relatives who gained a college education. After earning his degree, he returned to his home community to become principal, teacher, and coach at Homochitto High (the school long ago consolidated with Crosby High, which in the early sixties, consolidated with arch-rival Gloster High). The lay leader of Mt. Vernon Church, he was a tall, stately, serious minded and highly respected man. By the time Sonny Boy and I entered high school at Crosby, Cud'n J. C. had retired from teaching and was involved almost totally in farming and raising cattle. His was one of the few families in our community who owned horses.

Like the rest of us, Sonny Boy usually caught the "picture-show" bus which circulated through the community freely picking up passengers for the Saturday night western movie at the theatre in Crosby. And like the rest of us, he sometimes pretended to be Gene Autry, Roy Rogers, Lash Larue, Randolph Scott, or Johnnie Mack Brown – but with more authenticity – he owned a horse – and a saddle, something no other Poole boy could claim. Sonny Boy loved to ride his horse, which he did as often as Cud'n J. C. would release him from the corn field.

One hot July afternoon in about 1947 or 1948, J. C. had taken several cows to the sale in Liberty. A prized milk-cow tore out of the pasture and headed up the gravel road toward the Robertson's place. Sonny Boy Autry, then about 14 or 15 years old, quickly saddled his cow-roping pony and pursued the fleeing animal. He and his trusty companion caught up with the renegade on the Brushy Creek bridge, an arched, wooden span with bannisters, from which we all jumped into the cold water, some ten feet below, after a hot day's work. The courageous cowboy had a rope but decided not to use it. Instead, like the bull-dogging westerners on the silver screen at Crosby, he "dove" off his sprinting charger, aiming for the runaway cow's head. At that precise moment, the milk-producer, obviously realizing she had been overcome, decided to stop, turn around, and go back home. Sonny Boy missed bossy and bull-dogged the Brushy Creek bridge.

By the time J. C. returned from the cattle sale, the catapulting cowboy had been taken to Dr. David in Crosby, who had sewn up his numerous cuts, treated his multiple bruises, and encased his broken arm in plaster-of-paris. He was lying upon his bed, his left arm, stiffened by the cast, extending upward into the hot air of a house not yet blessed by the advent of air-conditioning, when his disconcerted Dad walked into the room. For a full minute, the two males faced each other without speaking a word – the suffering son and the dumbfounded dad. J. C. looked at his offspring's skinned feet, bare when he dismounted his mount, bandaged in white gauze, and his knees, both which clearly displayed several stitches. The father gradually moved his eyes up his son's midsection, now covered with tape and punctuated with stitches. He slid his gaze out to Sonny Boy's broken arm, slowly following it all the way to his finger-tips which protruded from the white cement. Then he retraced his visual steps back down his son's arm, across his battered chest up to his expressionless face which, like the rest of his bruised body, was covered with cuts. Finally, the tall, dignified, and mystified parent, looking directly into his elder son's blank face, quietly and reflectively broke the apprehensive silence.

"I DO believe I have SIRED an IDIOT."

THE RAM

Sonny Boy wasn't the only Poole who appeared to be an idiot because of a cow. I did too, although obviously my last name disqualifies me from claiming pure-Poole rights. It happened in the Summer of 1949. I was 14 years old and already a starter on the Crosby High football team, big for my age back then, a svelte 170 lbs.

Like Sonny Boy's situation, our best milk cow tore out of the pasture, too. Unlike Sonny Boy's situation, she was our ONLY milk cow. We sent word to all our relatives and neighbors throughout the community that the cow had gotten out and asked that they be on the lookout for her. About noon the mail-rider, sitting in his car at our mailbox, honked his horn.

Normally the mail-rider honking his horn offered good news – probably a package too big for the mailbox, so I sprinted barefoot the 30 yards from our front porch to his car.

"Paige!"

"Yes, Sir."

"Mr. Hollis waved me down and asked me to tell you that a cow had gotten into his pasture. He thought it may be y'alls."

"Yes, Sir, it probably is. I'll tell Mama Poole."

Mr. Hollis Seale was a strange man, at least to me, a mystical figure, seldom seen off his own farm, one of the few neighbors who never came to Mt. Vernon Methodist Church. Mama said the Seales were members of another church off somewhere which added to the mystery. Only rich folks could travel a distance to church.

Mr. Hollis differed from the rest of the Homochitto families another way too. He raised sheep, the only farmer in the community to do so. And he owned a ram, a big, mean-looking ram – with curved horns. I had seen the impressive creature many times from the school bus window, snorting, pawing the ground, chasing the ewes.

That's a mean animal," some school kid would comment almost every morning, as the bus rolled down the gravel road which circumvented Mr. Hollis' sheep pasture.

From Mama Poole's, the gravel road to Gloster and Crosby ran directly into the front of Mr. Hollis' house one mile away, where it then turned 90 degrees left, dropped down a hill for 200 yards, and turned 90 degrees right. The sheep pasture lay between the Seale home and the gravel road, which bordered the field on two sides. I hoped our cow had broken into one of Mr. Hollis' other fields and not the one containing the ram.

"Got your rope?" Mother called from the front porch as I started running toward the Seale's, wearing only a pair of UMAA athletic shorts, and barefoot. I turned my head back toward her and raised the rope, which I had coiled around my arm, above my head so she could see it. She waved and I kept jogging.

The mid-summer, high-noon sun splashed upon my thinly clad and darkened body like dirty dish water thrown from the kitchen door upon the bare ground. The few cumulus clouds were small patches of cotton pinned to a blue sheet, still, lifeless, anchored by stubborn air which refused to move. Like a great uncle blowing smoke rings from his corn-cob pipe, puffs of dust sprang from beneath my moving feet, and rocks on the gravel road challenged, uselessly, their hardened soles. Less than 10 sweaty minutes later I stood in front of Mr. Hollis.

I had never actually talked to Mr. Hollis alone, having seldom seen him that close. He was a large man dressed in over'hauls, as we Southerners often refer to them, about a two day's growth of beard upon his surprisingly friendly-looking face. He wore no shirt beneath the over'haul suspenders and an old felt hat, riddled with cut-out air vents, crouched upon his greying head. An encouraging twinkle brightened his eyes. Even so, I was a little apprehensive.

"How d'you do, Mr. Hollis?"

"Fine, son, how are you?"

"Fine. Mail-rider said our cow might be in your pasture."

"She might be. Walk right over here and you can see her, right down yonder," he pointed.

"Down yonder, Mr. Hollis? – down yonder in your sheep pasture?"

"Yeah – see her? – right yonder?" the old man pointed again.

"Yes, Sir, I see her. That's our cow alright. She in there with the ram?"

"Yeah, the ram's in there somewhere, maybe over on the backside."

"I've heard folks say that ram might be mean, Mr. Hollis," I pleaded, "reckon I oughta' go in there?"

"That ram won't bother you boy, he's a sheep. Sheep ain't mean. Now if he was a bull, you might want to worry 'bout him – but a ram? Naw, he won't bother you. Je'st go on in there and get your cow – that ram won't be no problem."

Mr. Hollis' eyes were still twinkling.

Fourteen year old Southern boys in 1949 neither argued with, nor doubted older men, not verbally, unless they were kin and prone to joking. If my uncles Buster and Ray, or great uncle Boss or Toad had told me what Mr. Hollis had just told me, I could be forgiven for wondering - but a stranger? A neighbor? I had no choice but to retrieve my cow. I could not call Mr. Hollis a liar.

"You can go through that gate right yonder, son. And after you get your cow, you can come back out the same way. The other gate is way down at the bottom of the hill."

"Yes, Sir."

I opened the gate and walked slowly down the inclined pasture toward my cow, who was grazing peacefully about two hundred yards away. Mr. Hollis leaned against the gate watching me. I couldn't see the ram although I did spot some ewes standing near a clump of trees about a hundred yards past ol' Shelly. I wanted to get a rope around the animal's neck as quietly as possible and get out of the pasture as quickly as possible. Although Mr. Hollis had convinced me the ram wasn't dangerous, I didn't want to test him. Maybe our primary source of milk will lend me a little cooperation, I hoped.

She didn't.

When I got within about 25 yards of my object, she jerked her head up, looked at me for a moment, lowed, turned and started trotting away.

I ran to her left, circled around her and turned her back toward the gate uphill. Mr. Hollis continued to watch – intently, still standing 30 degrees above me, 200 yards away.

Shelly started running again, and so did I – to head her off – several times. Each time I sprinted to get in front of her, I reduced the distance between us, until finally I dropped the noose around her neck. I had captured my prey and turned to lead her toward the gate where Mr. Hollis continued to stand, and watch.

Two important events occurred during my commotion with the cow. I became oblivious of everything except capturing her. And apparently the fuss attracted the attention of the ram, who must have been weathering the heat of the day in the clump of trees.

The sudden and intense pull upon the rope indicated quickly that all was not well. The intensifying sound of "clompity, clompity, clompity" provided the second clue. I turned my head toward the unnerving noise, yet confident in the assurances of the ram's owner, at the same moment my cow, who lacked my conviction, decided to desert me. "The approaching beast," I thought, "advanced only to inspect the invasion of his private domain." Running at half-speed he certainly seemed less than hostile, if not docile. My cow however, violently disagreed, and I suddenly found myself in a volcanic contest with a 400 lb. terrified animal. She had been too hard to capture to let her easily go. Stumbling but holding onto the rope, I focused all my attention onto her, assuming she offered my only REAL problem.

Shelly ripped the rough rope from my burning hands and I regained my balance just in time to realize that the clompity clomps had gotten much louder and with far less interval between them. I wheeled toward the charging brute, now no more than 10 yards away. He dropped his head and kept coming.   Balanced upon the precipice of indecision and doubt, I stood there, still believing in the innocence of his intentions.

The raging ram hit me just about my knees!

I gained neither psychological nor physical preparedness for the contact. All I had time to do was jump and I elevated my bare feet 6 inches off the ground before impact. The snorting ram ran directly under me. By the time his steel-plated head and rock-hard body cleared the spot where once I stood, my feet and head had exchanged positions – perfectly. I crumpled upon the heat soaked grassy ground like a country boy falling from a broken tree limb. I caught myself on my hands, rolled on my back through a pile of fresh cow manure, and scrambled to my feet in time to see the mad sheep stop, turn, snort, paw the ground, and from only 5 yards away charge again.

He hit me a second time.

The same things happened to me.

Mr. Hollis, leaning now upon the gate laughed deeply and profusely.

He hit me a third time.

The same things happened to me.

That old man, bending over, laughed more deeply and profusely, his body shaking with the glee of rural entertainment.

He hit me a fourth time.

The same things happened to me.

That idiot on the hill, now on his knees, was losing his breath.

I was too easy. By the time I extricated myself from the ground, my new and formidable foe would be upon me

173

again. Should I run? No, I can't outrun a ram. Should I drop a shoulder and take him on–? That was stupid. Should I side-step him? – jump to one side? Maybe. Surely when he lowers his head he can't see me. I need something to hit him with, a baseball bat – a two-by-four – a shotgun!

Twenty yards away, an old corn crib, or perhaps hay crib had fallen, a pool of clear water upon an arid desert, an armored car. Maybe I could run in increments to it, find a weapon and at last offer token defense, if not offense. The maneuver would have to be accomplished in several small moves. I couldn't get there in one sprint. I wouldn't have time. The ram would hit me from behind.

He hit me a fifth time.

I got off the ground and dashed five yards, turned and partially evaded my adversary, jumping to my left. He caught part of my right leg and flipped me again. I quickly arose from the turf and ran another five yards and repeated the tactic – and then another five yards – and then another five yards. On one knee and looking at the now fully-incensed creature, I groped behind me for the weapon. My fingers encircled a piece of wood, a two-by-four, about 3 feet long. I sprang to my feet, drew my bat back like Joe Dimaggio and when the speeding fast-ball got within 3 feet of me, I "swung" – from the ground. The two-by-four against the enemy's horns cracked like the sound of a whip. It accomplished nothing.

The battering ram hit me again.

Now smeared with the oil of pain and dangling from a rope of hopelessness, I knew I had to find SOME way to end the agony. Maybe, just maybe, instead of swinging a two-by-four into cyclops' head, I could swing my right arm under his neck and bull-dog him, like Sonny Boy intended to bull-dog his runaway cow. We weighed about the same!

Yeah! It might work, especially if I could flip him onto

his side and then fall on top of him. Running backs who crushed your helmet when hit head-on often went down easily when tackled from the side.

I got ready.

So did Bronko Nagurski. He snorted, pawed the ground and charged again.

I assumed my tackling stance, dropping my right hand to the ground, a fool about to attack a train – head on! Two yards away, the Cannonball Express dropped his head. I quickly stepped to my left and swung my right arm under the beast's neck and at the same time drove my right shoulder into his right side. Then I charged with all my strength, digging my bare toes into the grass covered ground. The attacker crashed to earth under my weight and I fell on top of him, a wrestler who finally threw his opponent, a defensive back who had been smeared for three and a half quarters, but managed a knock-out blow upon the fullback in the final minute of play, a tortoise who outran the hare.

My fallen antagonist struggled to rise against the force of my body, whimpered and lay still in defeat. But I wasn't satisfied. I locked my hands under the ram's neck, dug my knees into his side with all my weight upon them, and pulled with all my strength, wanting only to hear the sound of breaking bone.

The helpless assailant rolled his eyes and emitted a loud, shrill cry.

So did the frantic farmer, who by now had lost his glee and with rope in hand, dashed madly toward me. "PAIGE, PAIGE, DON'T KILL MY RAM – PAIGE, DON'T KILL MY RAM!"

Vengeance, soaked by fear, wrapped in anger, knows no compassion.

I felt two arms slip around my body. "Paige, don't kill

175

my ram. I've got a rope. I'll get him off of you."

"I'm gonna kill him, Mr. Hollis," I screamed, "besides, he ain't on me. I'm on him."

"I'll take care of him – just let him go – please."

I kept pulling.

"You get that rope around his neck, Mr. Hollis and I'll let him go, but I ain't gonna let him go 'til you do."

I felt the old man's arms loosen. Then he quickly tied the rope around his prize animal's head. I turned the ram loose, reluctantly, and stood to my feet. The whipped charger lay there, breathing heavily.

"You may have broken his neck, Paige."

"I hope I did break the son-of-a-bit – ah – gun's neck, Mr. Hollis," I retorted, as I brushed the grass and dirt off my sweaty body, "but I don't think I did. Did you see where my cow went?"

"Yes," he grunted and pointed. "She's right over there by the fence."

Indeed Shelly stood quietly by the fence, some 300 yards away, the rope still dangling from her brown neck, gazing mournfully in my direction. I walked slowly to her, reached down and grabbed the rope. She offered no resistance. "Um huh," I said. "You saw me whip that ram you were so afraid of, didn't you. Don't want none of ME, do you girl?"

Shelly's big brown eyes didn't reply.

A few minutes later, I unlatched the gate, led my troublemaker through it, and latched it again behind me. Only then did I glance toward the dynamic duo. The ram stood shakily on his feet and his relieved landlord seemed to be soothing the whipped animal's furrowed curved horn brow.

"Thank you, Mr. Hollis," I yelled and waved.

"You're welcome, son."

Twenty minutes later I led Shelly into our barnyard and took the rope off her neck. My mother, standing in the back yard, watched me move toward the well where I planned to draw some water and bathe.

"What happened to you, Son? And why is that cow manure all over your back?"

"Let me wash off some, Mother, and I'll tell you," I answered, "but you ain't gonna believe it."

"Don't say ain't, Son."

I told her the story. She believed it – just like I REAL-LY knew she would. Mothers always do.

Within a week or two, so did everyone else in the community.

Eight years later I pulled a Los Angeles Ram's helmet down hard upon my head and jogged proudly out upon their practice field for the first time. A thought suddenly coursed through my mind. "I'll bet I know better than all the rest of you why someone named a pro football team the Rams.

CHAPTER X

COACHES, WRITERS, AND COURAGEOUS PLAYERS

INTRODUCTION

I guess it was the times, but the relationships between coaches and writers, writers and players, and even players and coaches in the '50's seemed more informal, more relaxed, more fun, than they are today, even though a clear chain of command existed. The coaches exercised authority – without question – over the other two groups. And players, to some degree controlled the writers – for better or worse. As I mentioned in *Walk Carefully Around the Dead*, and in a following story, WE MADE IT, writers wrote something good about football players or they probably wrote nothing at all. But that rationale existed in an era when athletic lawsuits had yet to lay their oily heads upon the clean sheets of athletic sportsmanship. Principle prevailed over unearned material gain and writers REPORTED sports – they dared not try to control them, all the while maintaining professional integrity.

Coaches played tricks on writers and one another; writers played tricks on coaches and one another; and occasionally players discovered they could confront a coach and get by with it – with the coach's permission, of course.

GOLF IS A HEAVY GAME!

In *Walk Carefully Around the Dead*, I attempted to illustrate the two primary "sides" of Wobble Davidson, the long-time Ole Miss Freshman and red-shirt coach. To really appreciate him, both aspects must be understood. He possessed the ability to levy the harshest penalty upon a rebellious, dissipating football player while at the same time, causing the punished performer to laugh about it later – and to respect him – and to love him in spite of the chastening. Those two dimensions, though, involved vertical relationships, a coach who possessed and executed complete authority over his "subjects." But Wobble exhibited another capacity.

Intrinsic to his nature was the ability to both commit practical jokes upon his peers and take jokes from them. He could laugh as fully at himself when recipient of a prank as he could when committing one. That endowment served HIM well when he served Ole Miss as a member of Coach Vaught's staff. Rebel athletes often stood amazed when we heard of one coach pulling a mischievous trick upon another one. Somehow that failed to validate our concepts of the coaches' respect for one another, which we assumed they held, but it proved the presence of great senses of humor in all of them.

In the late 1950's, Wobble decided for the first time to begin playing golf. Almost all of Coach Vaught's staff played golf, and they played without cost on the old University Golf Course, located then west of Hemingway Stadium. Wobble walked and carried his clubs. The course owned no golf carts. He wanted the exercise anyway.

Soon the freshman coach, like many of the rest of us, became addicted to the game and early almost every morning he could be found out on the course, even during football season.

Chancellor Robert Khayat remembers, "Wobble would play golf almost every morning, carrying his clubs, walking. About the time he was becoming addicted to the game, Coach Bruiser Kinard found a piece of concrete just the right size, weighing about 20 lbs. Locating Wobble's golf bag one afternoon in the little pro-shop, Bruiser removed the clubs, inserted the perfectly fitting weight, and replaced the clubs."

Wobble carried the over-weight golf bag for about a week before mentioning his concern to his professional peers, all of whom had been closely observing.

"I don't know why," Wobble complained, "but for the last week or so I have really been tiring out playing golf. I can't understand it!"

"Hell, you're getting old," Bruiser commented. "That's what happens when you get old. You tire quicker!"

"I aged a hell of a lot in one week," responded the new golfer. "I didn't get this tired the FIRST few days I played!"

"I think you're sick," another coach advised. "You've looked a little pale for the last few days. If it was me, I think I'd go see the doctor."

"I think I might."

Two weeks later though, the suspicious freshman coach heard a rumor, emptied his clubs out on the pro-shop floor and discovered his sickness.

In true Wobble fashion, he thought the deed perpetrated upon him was hilarious, in part because he avoided a doctor bill.

> For when that Great Scorer comes
> To tell you of your fate,
> He'll not voice the score you shot
> But how you carried the weight!

WE MADE IT

Perhaps no relationship has changed more in the last thirty or forty years than the one between sports writer and athlete. Back in the Forties, Fifties and Sixties, writers wrote something good about athletes or they wrote nothing at all. Even a glancing examination of my scrapbook would lead you to believe I was Superman, Red Grange, George Patton and Billy Graham all rolled up into one. Even though my mother and I would like to have believed it, those close to me in my normal state knew better, my normal state being that which I lived when Mother wasn't around.

These days, of course, writers tend to record the truth, at least as they see it. If they miss veracity, they usually do so on the critical side, rather than the dispensable. As a group they seem to have little fear of being refused interviews, of receiving criticism themselves, or of being denied access into dressing rooms. But back in the early Sixties things were different.

Two veteran sportswriters for *The Clarion-Ledger* in those days were Carl Walters and Claude Sutherland. Both men were very capable pensmen and both were fortunate. They lived and worked only 150 miles from, and in the same state with, college football's winningest team, the Ole Miss Rebels. Both men enjoyed accessibility to abundant Rebel writing material but they longed to view, and to write about, Ole Miss football from a different panorama. They wanted to participate in a strategy meeting, where Coach Vaught and his staff presented to the team the offensive and defensive tactics for an upcoming opponent, any upcoming opponent. Understandably, however, those meetings, for obvious reasons, were closed to the public, especially the press, even trusted press.

For years, the twin reporters' promises of complete secrecy had failed to shift the adamant Coach from his immobile disposition. But one day their fortune was changed — by an unexpected phone call.

"Carl, this is John Vaught."

"How you doing, Coach?"

"Fine. How about you?"

"Great! What can I do for you?"

"You and Claude," Coach Vaught responded, "have been wanting to sit in on one of our strategy meetings for a good while. How about Monday?"

"Next Monday?"

"Yes!"

"We'll be there."

"Good! I know I can count on your secrecy!"

"You certainly can, Coach. We won't write about the meeting until after the game, and thanks."

All the way to Oxford, both writers reveled in their fortuity. "Can't believe we finally got to do this," Claude exclaimed to his traveling companion. "It's going to make a great story."

The two scribes reported to Coach Vaught. "The team's assembling in the dressing room now," the head mentor informed, "Go on in, speak to the players. The coaches and I will be in shortly."

The team, awaiting the coaches' entrance into the dressing room, was loud and clamorous. The two exhilarated writers sat in chairs to one side, jubilant that they had been granted access into the athletic "Holy of Holies," privy to intricate Ole Miss football strategies. No writer had ever been there.

The athletes suddenly grew silent. Coach Vaught and his staff entered the room.

"Men," Coach Vaught quietly implored, "as you know, this is a critical game for us. We've GOT to win it. So offense — defense — we're gonna do the same things this week that we did last week. DISMISSED! Let's go to work."

LOST TO A CHURCH

One of the most highly recruited quarterbacks ever to play high school football in the South was Steve Spurrier from Brentwood, Tennessee. Like Ollie Yates from Hattiesburg in 1953; Perry Lee Dunn from Natchez in 1961; and the Mannings, Peyton and Eli, dozens of schools were trying to sign him. Steve finally narrowed his list down to Ole Miss and Florida, and he declared his first choice to be the Rebels. John Cain and Junie Hovious recruited him, spending a lot of time in Brentwood.

Steve's first choice may have been Ole Miss but his dad's first choice lay with the first school which offered the best church.

I'll explain.

Brother Spurrier was a preacher and he presented to Coaches Hovious and Cain a most unusual offer.

During one of the final visits to Brentwood, the dad announced to Coach Cain, "Coach, Steve has narrowed his choice down to Ole Miss and Florida, and he's leaning toward Ole Miss. Now, his Mom and I want to live nearby. As you know, I'm a preacher. If you can find me a church either in, or near Oxford, I'm certain Steve will play for the Rebels. It doesn't have to be a huge church, an average size one will do. Do you think you can handle that?"

"I don't really know but I'll talk to Coach Vaught. We'll be in touch."

When Coach Cain got back to Ole Miss he presented Tom Swayze and Coach Vaught with Brother Spurrier's proposal.

"How in hell are we gonna find that man a church to preach in?" Swayze exclaimed. "We don't have any way to do that!"

"Maybe one of us ought to become a lay preacher and establish a system of finding churches," one of the coaches joked to the others.

"What's a lay preacher?" another asked.

Wobble playfully explained, "A preacher who lays everything in sight."

The staff agreed that the demand couldn't be met so Swayze sadly called Mr. Spurrier and gave him the bad news.

"I've lost a lot of boys to a lot of different things," recalled Coach Vaught, "but this is the first time I ever lost one to a church."

IT TOOK GUTS

I've heard this story several times and each time I stand amazed all over again. It doesn't compute easily in a brain which stood, and to some degree, still stands in awe of Coach John Vaught. Somewhere back in my childhood, long before I signed scholarship papers with Ole Miss, someone drove reverential respect for the head coach deeply into my sub-consciousness and it resides there still, embedded neither by my will nor against it. It seems to have been planted by a super-human force, an energy from a celestial world. I cannot envision myself reacting to Coach Vaught like blocking back Buddy Bowen did in the fall of 1947. Bill Stribling, Buddy's teammate, tells the story.

"We were playing Tulane in New Orleans," related Bill, "and Coach Vaught, much to our surprise, announced that he would conduct no bed-check after the game."

I can understand Bill's amazement. In four years at Ole Miss, the head coach loosened the reins of dissipation only once. Like all of us, Buddy took advantage of it.

Ole Miss had traveled to the Crescent City on the train – the City of New Orleans. The players were to assemble at the train station on Sunday morning for the trip home. No one, and that included All-Americans Charlie Conerly and Barney Poole, dared miss that muster – no one that is, except Buddy.

"Buddy, like many of the rest of us had just returned to Ole Miss from the War," continued Bill. "He wasn't at assembly and he wasn't on the train. To make matters even worse, no one on the team had seen him Saturday night – had no idea where he was."

All the players grew extremely worried about the blocking back, not so much because he couldn't take care of himself, though – he had survived World War II – but because they were certain Coach Vaught was going to kick him off the team.

"He wasn't on the train," remembered Bill. "We knew he was in serious trouble."

Monday morning Buddy, from a distance, watched Coach Vaught and his staff arrive at their offices. A minute or two later, he stormed angrily into the head coach's office.

"Why in hell did-ja' leave me, Coach? I had a helluva' time getting back up here!"

"He chewed Coach Vaught out for leaving him," mused Bill. And Coach let him stay on the team. We couldn't believe it."

I'll bet that was a lone anomaly.

"We never did find out where he'd been," reflected his teammate. "But I found out one thing – the best defense is a good offense."

Humph! That may still be true.

IT WON'T DO RIGHT

Even today it's very difficult for many of us who played football at Ole Miss under Wobble Davidson to envision him drinking alcohol. Somehow in our conditioned minds, the coach and "drink" stand miles apart, divided by his total dedication to seeing that, as players, we didn't do it. So when those of us who lived in accumulative fear at being caught by him hear of his drinking, we must first recondition our minds to the fact that he occasionally imbibed, before the story itself amuses us. That's not often easy.

After Wobble left the Ole Miss coaching staff he scouted for the Dallas Cowboys. The new job forced him to travel extensively, visiting college coaching staffs, football practices and games. He spent many nights during the football season in hotels, and occasionally he would visit the bar before retiring to his room.

Such was the case one night in a college town somewhere when he had a little too much to drink, a very rare occurrence for Wobble.

"He had consumed more than usual," one of his dearest friends and admirers admitted to me, "and he was a little unstable on his feet. He drank a number of exotic-type drinks, with vermouth, which of course often produces a dryness in the mouth."

The NFL scout teetered to his room, slowly undressed, turned his light off and fell into bed. A while later extreme thirst awakened him. Holding onto the revolving wall and the rotating chair, he groped his way to the bathroom, enabled by the dim outside light which filtered into his room around the drapery.

"When Coach got to the bathroom," his friend continued, "he picked up a glass in the pale light and tried in vain to fill it with water. But he was holding the glass upside down. Eventually he realized THAT, and turned it over but he didn't know the glass was covered with cellophane. With some concern, he finally gave up."

Having failed to quench his thirst, the worried scout retraced his unsteady steps to the bed, flipped on the light, picked up the telephone and with great anxiety, called home.

"Sara, I think I'm going crazy! I can't get water to go into the drinking glass!!"

As a retired marriage counselor I would love to have heard her wifely reply, and to have seen the expression on her face.

Years later the former Ole Miss football coach was still laughing about the time "I went crazy in a hotel room."

IT'S TIME THAT YOU GOT UP

One of Mississippi's most prolific sports storytellers is, and has been for years, Jimmy McDowell, long-time sports writer and retired director of the National Collegiate Football Hall of Fame. In the Spring of 1996, Ray and Wanda Poole, my wife, Jimmy and I were visiting in his hotel room in Jackson. We were in town to play in the NFL Player's Association Golf Tournament the next day and we were spinning tales. Jimmy told one about Fred Russell, the long-time sports writer of *The Nashville Banner* newspaper.

I've repeated the story to countless numbers of people since hearing it from the mouth of the master. I have never finished telling it without interrupting myself with my own laughter. I already know I'll laugh all the way through the writing of it. At least I won't drown out its telling for you.

It seems Fred was in Atlanta covering a sports event. He was sitting in the lobby of his hotel early one morning near the front desk reading the paper and enjoying a cup of coffee.

His attention was averted by a commotion at the desk.

"Young man," screamed a plump and very angry woman, "I'm Mrs. Johnson in room 531. You were to give me a wake-up call at 6:30 this morning. YOU DID NOT and I'm going to be late for a business meeting. I'M TELLING YOU NOW – I WANT A CALL AT 6:30 TOMORROW MORNING and if I do not get it, you're going to be very, very sorry. DO YOU UNDERSTAND?"

"Yes, Ma'am," the embarrassed young clerk quietly replied, as the seething businesswoman scurried through the front door of the hotel.

That night, Fred set his alarm clock for 6:00 a.m. When it went off, he quickly brushed his teeth, dressed and at 6:15 he dialed room 531. "Mrs. Johnson, this is the front desk. It's 6:30 AND TIME YOU GOT YOUR FAT ASS OUT OF BED!"

The mischievous troublemaker then hustled down to the lobby, bought a newspaper behind which he partially hid his face, and waited. A minute or two later, a robed, tousled-haired, enraged Mrs. Johnson burst through the elevator doors and headed for the innocent, unsuspecting, and soon-to-be attacked young man behind the counter.

The roguish writer observed with pleasure from his 50-yardline seat.

YOU NOT GOING, SLICK?

Before this story can be funny to you, two facts must be established. First, when John Vaught was head coach at Ole Miss, he, like a giant mama eagle, ruled the athletic roost. Although the players may not have feared him in the same manner we trembled at the wrath of Wobble, we certainly never challenged him. In my four years at Ole Miss, I heard no syllable of protest by a player against Coach Vaught; I recall

189

no voice of negativism toward him even in the closed door sanctity of the dormitory, where tired and battered players were wont to gather for that purpose; and no one EVER called him by his nickname to his face – SLICK – until Hobby Horse.

I'm not certain how the players came to nickname Coach Vaught "Slick." It may have been his "laid back" style of coaching or his smooth, yet commanding voice, but every time a player used it, he looked over his shoulder to make sure no one in authority heard, especially Coach Vaught.

Frankly, I never could coerce myself to call him Slick, even behind his back. I always got caught when I did anything wrong, whether I executed it in secret or not. The benefit my masculinity might have gained from voicing it wasn't worth the risk. But several players discovered either enough courage or innocence to do it. Frank "Hobby Horse" Halbert was one of them though obviously, he had never called Coach Vaught "Slick" to his face, being neither that brave nor ignorant – until the situation demanded it.

Frank Halbert provides the second important fact in this tale.

When Frank was a student at Ole Miss in the late nineteen-fifties, college football teams were allowed to sign as many football players as their athletic budgets would allow, the balance sheet, rather than the NCAA determining it. So Ole Miss signed 60 to 100 football players each year. Occasionally one would be signed who stood little chance of becoming a starter but whose personality, energy and esprit-de-corps were needed additions to the team's morale. Hobby Horse was such a player, a "good" running back, signed out of Aberdeen High, about five feet, eight inches tall and 175 lbs. But he faced the misfortune of playing at Ole Miss when you needed to be a "great" running back just to make the traveling squad.

Ole Miss was practicing for the 1958 Sugar Bowl game. The final practice in Oxford had ended and the team members were waiting in the bleachers, which filled one entire side of the varsity dressing room. The turbulent athletes suddenly grew mute as the Head Coach entered the room for final traveling instructions.

"Fellows," Coach Vaught began, "the first thing I want to do today is appoint the traveling squad. I will call out the names of the players making the trip."

Intently, each player listened for his name. When Coach Vaught finished, Frank's name had not been called. Gently Coach Vaught turned toward the yet hopeful halfback. "Frank, I'm gonna miss you tomorrow."

"What's the matter, Slick, you not going?"

When the team's laughter finally subsided, an amazed and impressed Head Coach added one player to the traveling roster. Hobby Horse became a permanent fixture.

"How could you leave a fellow with that much courage and that quick a mind behind?" Coach Vaught later asked, with a huge grin.

CHAPTER XI

HE MADE IT – HE MADE IT!

In 1967, I staged a comeback. I made it!!! Oh, not the comeback – I made it another way as a result of attempting the comeback! My comeback failed. I'll explain!

I was the first football player signed by the New Orleans Saints, mentioning the event in another chapter – One Reason I Hate LSU. While at the Saints training camp, I was introduced to a new piece of strengthening equipment, the Exergenie, a rope pulled through a metal tube, controlled by settings. Handles attached to both ends of the rope, according to the makers of the device, advertised that it offered both an isotonic and an isometric exercise. Two people used it at one time, one pulling the rope and one feeding it through the apparatus. The partner "feeding" the rope through the Exergenie had to feed it gradually and continuously. Empowered by the series of small pulleys inside the tube, the "feeder" could actually stop the movement of the rope with two fingers.

After the Saints cut me, I bought one of the gadgets and brought it back to Eupora, where I lived. I liked working out on it, because it could be used to exercise every muscle in the body.

A friend, Rusty Denman, my attorney, and I jogged several miles each day. Then we worked out on the Exergenie. The combination afforded us a great workout.

I was standing on the board to which the Exergenie was attached, and I was lifting in a simulated full press, like a weightlifter lifting heavy weights from the floor to above his head. Rusty was holding his handle in his right hand and controlling the movement of the rope through the Exergenie with his left hand. Between his left and right hands, the rope sagged.

A mutual friend walked into the room. Without thinking, Rusty released the rope with his left hand and greeted the newcomer but he held onto the handle with his right hand. That allowed me to quickly pull the sagging rope through the machine until his right hand, which was grasping the handle, suddenly stopped me. I was bending over. The pain emanating from my back propelled me to the floor.

Rusty apologized.

I lay there for 30 minutes or so before I painfully arose.

The next day I noticed blood when I went to the bathroom – both ways.

I got a little worried. Even though I believed Denman "done" it, I went to my doctor, Bill Gifford, in Eupora. Another friend had recently died of colon cancer. Passed blood, which he ignored, had been a sign.

"It's probably caused by the injury, Paige," Bill speculated," but to be on the safe side, I'm going to make you an appointment with a specialist in Jackson to check your kidneys and your colon. When can you go?"

"Just make the appointment, Bill. I'll adjust."

I checked into the Baptist Hospital late in the afternoon. It was the late 60's.

Before long a nurse entered my room. She held up a flask-looking object.

"You want me to do this, or can you do it?" she gruffly asked.

"What?"

"This enema! You want me to do it, or can you do it?"

"Why do either one of us have to do it?"

Anger flashed in her eyes!

"Why do we have to do it?" she asked, her raised voice reflecting disbelief. "To clean you out!! That doctor's not gonna wade through a filthy tunnel."

"I'll be dirty again in the morning."

"How's that?" she screeched.

"After I eat supper tonight and breakfast in the morning."

I was pleased that I could exhibit my knowledge of the human waste system, especially to an expert.

"You're not gonna eat supper tonight, nor breakfast in the morning."

"I'M NOT gonna EAT SUPPER TONIGHT, NOR BREAKFAST IN THE MORNING? I wish someone had told me!"

"Why?"

"I'd have eaten more lunch," I declared emphatically.

"You won't starve. Have you had an enema before?"

"I don't think so. I can't remember."

"You'd remember it! You want me to do it or you want to do it?"

Tough decision! I had no desire to puncture myself, but I didn't trust her. The anger and frustration still marked her stern face.

"Can you show me how?"

Ten minutes later, she concluded, "You've got to keep doing it 'till it comes out clear. Then call me. I'll need to see it."

"Figures," I groaned.

"The doctor will see you in the morning." She didn't smile.

THE DAY

"Good morning, Paige. How are you feeling this morning?" the doctor inquired. A nurse stood beside him, her hand resting on the cart which she had pushed into my room, a funny-looking piece of equipment on top of it. She smiled a smile of friendliness, I thought then. Later I realized it was probably a smile of sympathetic compassion, or maybe glee.

The doctor was a tall, slim man with a merciful face, a twinkle in his eyes. His short hair was grey, and he spoke with a soft, deliberate voice. His demeanor reflected knowledge.

I needed that!

"I saw the Cotton Bowl game," he declared.

"When we played TCU?"

"Yes. Great game."

"You go to Ole Miss?" I hopefully asked.

"Many years before you got there. By the way, you did a good job last night."

"Last night. I did?"

"When you gave yourself the enema. The nurse told me you did a good job."

"Didn't want you to have to wade through a dirty tunnel, Doctor. Ole Miss people help each other!"

He didn't answer.

"Have you eaten anything, Paige?"

"Not since noon yesterday, Doc. I'm starving."

"It won't be long," he assured. "Now I want to explain today's procedure. I'm going to check your colon here in your room..."

"How long will that take?" I interrupted.

"Not long," he continued. "Then we'll take you to the x-ray room to complete the examination."

It sounded simple and innocent enough. I lost some of my fear.

"Now, Paige, I want you to get on the bed and lie on your stomach."

I tried to hold the hospital gown in place as I climbed onto the bed. It was hard to do.

"Now, get up on your knees and put your head on your pillow."

I glanced at the grinning nurse. She seemed disinterested.

"Is she gonna be in here, Doc?"

"The nurse? Of course. She's my assistant."

I grew self-conscious.

"Paige, I'm gonna insert a tube. Through it, I'll be able to inspect your colon. Are you ready?"

"I don't know. How big is it?"

"The tube? Not big. It won't hurt," he assured.

"Turn it on," the doctor instructed the nurse. I thought he meant the machine which rested on the table. The nurse walked over to my television set and turned it on – loud.

I got worried.

"Here goes, Paige," the doctor warned.

I felt the cold of the metal.

"You could at least have warmed it up, Doc."

"Sorry."

"That's o.k.," I groaned as I felt the doctor push on the tube.

"GOSH, DOC, how BIG is that thing?"

"Am I hurting you?" he asked.

"Yes! I'm not used to this."

"I hope not," he responded.

"That thing's got to be huge."

"Why do you say that? Are you hurting?"

"Yes – that and the echo."

"The echo?" the doctor queried. "What echo?"

"When you talk, I can hear an echo. You got your head up in there?"

He didn't answer.

I looked back at the nurse. She was still smiling.

A life-time later, I felt the tube slide out.

"I know what it's like now, to have a baby," I authoritatively declared.

"No, you don't!" the nurse countered. She had stopped smiling.

"Take him to x-ray, Nurse," the doctor commanded.

The female assistant looked at me. "You want to walk or you want me to get you a wheelchair?"

"I'll walk. I don't think I can sit right now!"

THE WALK

"How far we got to go?" I asked as the nurse and I stepped out into the brightly-lit hall. With my left hand I held the two sides of my hospital gown together in the rear. Soft music floated down from the speakers in the ceiling. My bare feet squeaked against the tile floor.

"Not far – about 200 feet, I guess."

The smile had re-surfaced on my nurse's face. I quickly acquired the sense that I was marching to a serious destination, being led by a scout. I tried not to walk in cadence with the music.

We had traveled only a short distance when I noticed people looking at me, examining me from top to bottom with their medical eyes. Nurses paused from their duties, moved over against the wall and looked. I could feel their gaze still upon me as I passed. Other nurses stuck their heads out of rooms and watched. Several cleaning people stopped mopping and let us pass, leaning upon their mops and watching me all the way down the hall. The two doctors we met, moved over against the wall and let us pass, their eyes locked on me.

I spoke to them. They nodded, and I heard one of them say to the other after we had passed, "Looks pretty firm. I believe he can."

"I don't know," the other one whispered.

"What did that doctor mean, Nurse? 'I believe he can.'"

"I didn't hear it, Mr. Cothren. Probably talking about another doctor's skill, or something. Maybe a golfer."

"Why are all these people looking at me?"

"What people?" my co-walker asked.

"All these people – these nurses, and doctors. Even the cleaning people!"

"You paranoid?"

"No," I emphatically replied. "I'm not paranoid."

"Well, if they are looking at you, it's probably because you played football. Didn't you play football?"

"Well, yes," with a touch of 'hidden' pride, I answered.

"Who for?"

"Ole Miss, the L.A. Rams, and the Philadelphia Eagles."

"Well, that is probably why they looked at you. Not every day do we have a football star in here."

"I don't know," I softly argued. "I don't believe all those people could be football fans. Besides I heard them all whispering as I passed. Sounds like some were saying "yes" and some were saying "no.""

"Now I know you're paranoid, Mr. Cothren."

"Paige," I corrected.

"What?"

"Just call me Paige. I'm not old enough to be Mr. Cothren."

"Well — Paige — here we are."

We turned into the x-ray room, and as we did I glanced back down the hall. Numerous eyes still gazed at me.

I got worried again.

THE X-RAY ROOM

"Come in, Mr. Cothren. You are in x-ray," another nurse invited. "Have you ever had the barium x-ray before?"

"Well, I had x-rays on my broken hand, my cheek bone, my —."

"No, no! What I'm asking is have you ever had the BARIUM x-ray procedure?"

"I don't know what that is," – I heard the doubt in my own voice. "I just thought I was going to be x-rayed."

"Well, you are," the nurse explained, "but it's a little more complicated than that. Your doctor will be here in a minute or two, and he'll explain it to you. You can go ahead and get up on the table."

I had two goals as I prepared to climb up on the x-ray table – hold my gown together in the back and mount it athletically. After all I was a pro football player.

"On my stomach or on my back?" I asked her.

"On your back."

I pulled my gown down as far as it would go, and I felt the cold of the table against my back side. The x-ray machine hovered over me like a prison sentry standing over an inmate. The spot-lights, blazing from the ceiling, blinded me. I folded one arm over my closed eyes and waited – but not long.

I heard the sound of several shoes on the tile floor. Two men and another nurse entered the room. Both men were doctors. They introduced themselves to me. The four of them surrounded the x-ray table.

"Paige, have you ever had the barium x-ray procedure before?" one of the doctors asked. He was the big one. He smiled when he asked me the question.

"I don't think so, Doctor."

"That most likely means you haven't. Folks tend to remember it," his smile suggesting knowledge I didn't have.

The smaller doctor and the two nurses nodded in agreement, their faces stern looking. Like the people in the hall, they seemed to be sizing me up.

"What is this barium x-ray, doctor? Are you going to explain it to me?"

"Yes. We are going to insert a tube up your rectum and,"——

"Up my rectum? You're gonna put another tube up my rectum? I thought I was just gonna get x-rayed!"

"You are," the big doctor softly explained, "but we have to get the barium into the lower part of your body. In order to do that we have to insert the tube. It doesn't hurt."

"That's what the last doctor who stuck something up me said."

"Well, this doesn't hurt. We have to pump a good bit of barium, which is a thick liquid, into you and look at you through the x-ray. That's how we can tell if you have any kind of growth —"

"How much barium you gonna pump in me?"

"A good bit. You will feel real full, and it will be a little hard for you to hold the barium in, but you have to – 'til we get through looking at you through the x-ray. Then we'll let you off the table, and you can empty it out."

"Where?"

"That commode right there." He pointed toward the wall behind me.

I sprang up on one elbow, looked behind me and saw it – a commode just like he said, against the wall – in the open x-ray room – in plain view.

"You mean I'm gonna just get up off this x-ray table, walk over to that commode and use it in plain view of everyone? Why don't you let me go to the bathroom?"

"Well, uh, uh, Paige, we try to get you to the toilet as soon as we can when we finish with you. Some people can't quite make it to the bathroom. We wanted to make the procedure as convenient for you as possible."

One of the nurses snickered. I don't think she meant to–!

I got worried again.

"Let's get started," the big doctor suggested. A nurse started folding my hospital gown up toward my head. I tried to hold it down.

"Wait a minute," I yelled. "I don't have anything on under this!"

She didn't stop. The gown finally ended up folded under my chin. I think I blushed.

"Paige, you'll have to put your feet in these stirrups," one of the doctors ordered.

By that time most of the fight had left me; most of the dignity, too. I blindly obeyed.

I heard a motor running.

"What's that sound, Doctor?"

"That's a pump," he murmured.

"What's it for?"

"To pump the barium into you."

"Oh – you need a pump for that?"

"Of course," with a touch of apparent frustration in his voice, the doctor answered. I could feel four sets of impatient eyes resting on me, hopefully on my face, probably not. They weren't going to be working on my face. I tried not to think about it.

"Now, Paige, "I'm inserting the tube. Relax."

"I'm trying!"

"You will feel the barium being pumped into you."

"You're right about that, doctor!"

"Now when we get the barium into you, I will—"

"DOCTOR, YOU'RE PUMPING TOO MUCH INTO ME."
I looked down toward my swelling stomach.

"No, we aren't," the doctor quickly countered.

"But I can see my stomach rising —! I can't even see my pen–,ah, ah, my private part anymore."

"It's still there," a nurse assured me. I looked at her. She wasn't smiling. The other nurse giggled. They both grabbed my arms, one each.

"Doc, Doc, you're pumping too much in me!!"

"No, I'm not – now what I was about to say is when we get the barium into you" —

"Doc, I'm telling you – you're putting too much in me – I'm warning you!" I screamed.

"—then I'll take the tube out and look at you through the x-ray."

"Doc, you're making a big mistake!"

I felt the tube slide out. I also felt the barium trying to —!

"Doc, I can't hold it!"

"You've got to hold it. I have to look through the x-ray. Now, Paige, Dr. Johnson is going to press on your stomach a little—"

"Why?" I frantically asked.

"To move the barium into every part of your body while I look at it through the x-ray."

I felt a 500-pound hand push down on my stomach.

"STOP, DOCTOR, STOP – I can't hold it."

I looked into the faces of the restraining nurses for help. One of them looked me directly in the eye. She seemed to really mean it when she barked, "You've GOT to hold it, Paige – now HOLD it!"

"I'm trying," I whimpered. I wondered what she would do to me if I didn't.

"How much longer, doctor?" I begged.

"Not long."

"How long?" The 500-pound hand was bouncing my stomach up and down like a Boston Celtic guard dribbling a basketball. The doctor didn't answer.

"I'm not kidding, doctor. I can't hold it!"

He still didn't answer.

"Doc —!"

"We're almost through, now. Hang on," the doctor looking through the machine finally assured me. Dr. Johnson kept jumping up and down on my intestines. The muscles necessary to contain the barium were weakening fast.

"Doctor, I'm not playing — I CAN'T HOLD IT — I MEAN IT – I CAN'T HOLD IT." The clock on the wall told me I had lain on the table, full of barium, for twenty minutes. It seemed like twenty hours.

"You don't have to anymore," I heard the doctor say. "GO."

One of the nurses repeated the doctor's command, "GO!"

Holding my gown above my inflated middle, I sprinted the four yards to the splendid, exhibited commode and jumped bottom first onto it at exactly the same moment the barium exploded from me. I felt no shame—!

"HE MADE IT, HE MADE IT," the nurse who had issued the command to go, screamed, as she looked first at the smiling, examining doctor, and then toward the open doorway leading out into the hall. I jerked my head toward the door. Standing there were two female nurses and a man who appeared to be a doctor, big smiles on their faces. "HE MADE IT – HE MADE IT," they repeated, as they moved abruptly away from the doorway. From farther down the hall, someone else repeated the refrain, "HE MADE IT," and then another, and another, until twenty voices all up and down the hall echoed the chorus — "HE MADE IT!"

Relief came quickly on that porcelain throne. With satisfied ease, I looked back at the four who had just moments before been my adversaries. Contrasted with the two who were smiling, stood the "mighty masher" and his disconsolate companion. Both exhibited looks of dejection. My examining doctor walked around the x-ray table, looked Dr. Johnson directly in the eye, held out his hand, palm up and said, "Do I know tight cheeks or what! You owe me five dollars."

Ms. Nurse Smiles looked at Ms. Nurse Melancholy, held out her hand, and repeated the doctor's reminder.

By that time I was looking for the paper. I had difficulty mentally assimilating what I had just heard. "You mean you bet on me making it to the commode?"

The winning physician sauntered over to where I still manned my relief seat, looked down into my appeased eyes and reflected, "Made five dollars off you! Do I know tight cheeks or what?"

"Were the four of you the only ones who bet?" I asked, my new-found respite eliminating concern one way or the other.

"NO!", Ms. Nurse Melancholy disgustedly replied, as she scurried toward the door. "Why do you think all those people were looking at you in the hall? — your FOOTBALL??"

CONCLUSION

How does a writer conclude a book, or two books, which have no end, stories which never stop? How can I declare these tales to be a termination of athletic humor at Ole Miss? A finale of fun? – an extinction of athletic mirth? As long as young men and women submit themselves to the authority of coaches and to the rigors of athletic competition, humorous actions and confrontations will be engineered, remembered, related, and laughed about, especially by those who either experienced them or who enjoyed membership in the experiencing generation. Somehow yarns exhibit more importance to those of the same era in which the fables occurred. Perhaps someone who wore the red and blue from the decades of the 70's and 80's and now the 90's may decide to record the comical incidents endemic to those eras – and those of another age, like me, will enjoy them.

Mentioning this once in *Walk Carefully Around the Dead*, I refuse to buffet your minds with another extended soliloquy. However, please permit me to bore you with an abbreviated one – I received a great blessing from writing these two books, *Walk Carefully Around the Dead* and *An Academy Called Pain.*

An old and dear friend once counseled me, "Paige, if you really want to leave something which will be remembered by succeeding generations, leave it in print, not on tape." I've decided to do just that. The gracious owners of several Mississippi bookstores have exhorted me to continue writing. Emphasizing this challenge, one promised, "As fast as you'll write 'em, we'll sell 'em."

By the Lord's Grace, I'm gonna keep writing 'em.

A SPECIAL "THANK YOU"

To those who contributed stories:

Billy Ray Adams	Bobby Fisher
Warner Alford	Louis Guy
Buddy Alliston	Buddy Harbin
Bo Ball	Robert Khayat
Don Barkley	Kent Lovelace
Bob Benton	Worthy McClure
Gayle (Tar-Baby) Bowman	Jimmy McDowell
Ray Brown	Joe Pasley
Jack Cavin	Richard Price
Hanson (Bull) Churchwell	Dicky Smith
Art Doty	Bill Stribling
Gene Dubuisson	Claude Sutherland
Jim Dunaway	Richard Weiss
Doug Elmore	Melvin Wilson
Chubby Ellis	

To Ann Randle Vanderbeek: a Mississippi State graduate who momentarily cast off her Maroon and White cloak of confrontation and donned the Red and Blue of deep friendship – for typing the manuscript.